Famous Footballers of Wales

Famous Footballers of Wales

Dean Hayes

Aureus

First Published 2001

©2001 Dean Hayes

Dean Hayes has asserted the Author's right under the Copyright, Designs and Patents Act 1988 to be identified as Author of this Work.

All rights reserved. No part of this publication may be reproduced, stored in a retrieval system, or transmitted, in any form or by any means, electronic, mechanical, photocopying or otherwise, without the prior permission of Aureus Publishing.

ISBN 1 899750 21 5

Printed in Great Britain.

A catalogue record for this book is available from the British Library.

Aureus Publishing Limited, 24 Mafeking Road, Cardiff, CF23 5DQ, UK.
Tel: (029) 2045 5200 Fax: (029) 2045 5200
Int. tel: +44 29 2045 5200 Int. fax: +44 29 2045 5200
E-mail: sales@aureus.co.uk
          meuryn.hughes@aureus.co.uk
Web site: www.aureus.co.uk

Acknowledgments

The author wishes to thank the following organisations for their help in producing this book:

The Football League; The Association of Statisticians; The British Newspaper Library; National Library of Wales; Harris Reference Library; Clwyd Record Office and the Central Reference Libraries of Blackburn, Bolton, Cardiff, Liverpool, Manchester, Swansea and Wrexham.

Thanks also to the following individuals:

Gareth Davies; Richard Evans; Tom Griffiths; Ben Hayes; David Higson; Gareth Jones; Glyn Jones; Iain Price and Harry Williams.

The photographs in this book have been supplied by the Manchester Evening News, the Liverpool Daily Post and Echo, the Bolton Evening News, the Lancashire Evening Post and from the author's personal collection.

Introduction

Many famous footballers have been produced by Wales, among them, Billy Meredith, John Charles, Ivor Allchurch, Ian Rush and Ryan Giggs.

The talent to play football is a timeless quality. All that changes is the fitness level, tactics and techniques, but it is impossible to measure accurately quality and skill. That is why in the end, it is a matter of personal choice and certainly not everyone will agree with my choice of Wales' most famous fifty footballers. In making my selections, I have considered my own personal recollections, the statistical side of a player's career and in nearly all cases, I think I have recognised that a famous player needs a good supporting cast.

During my research it became obvious as to why facts and figures are a source of argument and frustration. Even when every effort has been made to get the details correct, they could still be wrong, as, in some instances, there are no means of double checking. Often discrepancies do not come to light until a player's career total of appearances and goals scored is added up - this could well be years after the circumstances of disputed goals have been forgotten. However, everything possible has been done to ensure the facts in this book are correct.

For me, it has been a pleasure to have seen most of these famous names in Welsh football play and to those who I have not included in my final fifty - Dai Astley, Clayton Blackmore, Mark Bowen, Terry Hennessey, Barry Horne, John Mahoney, Gil Reece and Stuart Williams - I would say it is their omission that will generate the biggest debate among readers of this book.

Dean P. Hayes

IVOR ALLCHURCH

Birthplace	Swansea
Born	16 December 1929
Died	9 July 1997

Football League Career

	Appearances	Goals
Swansea City	446(2)	165
Newcastle United	143	46
Cardiff City	103	39

68 caps - 23 goals
(Swansea Town)
1951 : v England, N.Ireland, Portugal, Switzerland
1952 : v England, Scotland, Rest of UK, N.Ireland
1953 : v Scotland England, N.Ireland, France, Yugoslavia
1954 : v England, Scotland N.Ireland, Austria
1955 : v Yugoslavia, Scotland, England, N.Ireland
1956 : v England, Scotland, Austria, N.Ireland
1957 : v Scotland, England
1958 : v Israel(2) N.Ireland, Hungary(2), Mexico, Sweden, Brazil
1959 : v (Newcastle United) v Scotland, England, N.Ireland
1960 : v England, Scotland
1961 : v N.Ireland, Spain(2) Hungary
1962 : v England, Scotland, Brazil(2) Mexico

(Cardiff City)
1963 : v Scotland, Hungary(2) England, N.Ireland
1964 : v England
1965 : v Scotland, England, Greece, N.Ireland, Italy, USSR

(Swansea Town)
1966 : v England, USSR, Scotland, Denmark, Brazil(2) Chile

Known as the 'Golden Boy of Welsh Football', Ivor Allchurch was one of the most gifted players ever to emerge from Wales. He had been discovered in youth football by Swansea's Joe Sykes and recruited to the ground staff at the Vetch Field. His league debut came at West Ham United on Boxing Day 1949 after which he began to develop a fine understanding with Welsh international Billy Lucas who was by now playing at half-back. Allchurch at inside-left had all the grace and timing of an experienced player and he used the space that Lucas created to lay on pin-point passes for the goalscoring opportunities.

Despite only having appeared in 30 league games for the Swans, Wales capped him in November 1950 against England at Sunderland. Wales lost 4-2 with Trevor Ford scoring both the Welsh goals but the selectors decided that Allchurch was the man to fill the role vacated by Bryn Jones who had played his last international two years before. Indeed, that match against England was to be the first of twenty-seven consecutive games that Allchurch was to play for Wales during the next six seasons.

During the 1950-51 season, Allchurch became the youngest Swansea Town player to have appeared in all 42 league matches during the campaign. The following season he was selected to play for the Welsh League against the Irish League, scoring two and making three in an easy win at Windsor Park. First Division clubs were now beginning to take an interest in the blond youngster and Wolves made an abortive £36,000 offer for the gifted inside-forward.

Allchurch was a fixture in the Welsh team, missing only a handful of games through injury. One of his best games for Wales was against a combined United Kingdom side for the 75th Anniversary of the Football Association of Wales when he scored twice in a 3-2 win.

Back at the Vetch Field, Allchurch netted the first of seven hat-tricks for the Swans in April 1953 against Brentford and his second twelve months later at Fulham. In 1954-55, Allchurch was the club's leading scorer with 20 goals including a hat-trick in the 6-1 defeat of Ipswich Town. The club's first match that season saw Allchurch chalk up another record. For some reason, the Swans' opening game started fifteen minutes before the remainder of the Football League matches which were played that day. The visitors West Ham United were beaten 5-2 with Allchurch scoring that season's first Football League goal ! In 1955-56 he netted another hat-trick in a 5-1 win at Notts County, his first goal coming within a minute of the kick-off. During the 1956-57 season, he scored a goal in each of nine consecutive League and Cup matches. When Derby County were beaten 7-0 in April 1958, Allchurch netted another treble and four months later, he scored four goals in a 5-0 win over Sunderland who had just been relegated from the First Division.

Though Ivor was a more gifted player than his younger brother Len, the two of them wore a Welsh shirt against Northern Ireland in 1955 in a game which also saw Wales field another pair of brothers in John and Mel Charles. That year also saw Ivor Allchurch play his part in Wales' 2-1 win over England at Ninian Park as they gave one of their best-ever team displays. After he had appeared for Wales in the 1958 World Cup Finals in Sweden, he received great praise from the World's Press and it was obvious that he would soon get the chance to show what he could do in the top flight.

Newcastle United signed him for £28,000 in October 1958 and he made a great start for the Magpies, scoring twice in a 3-1 win over Leicester City. When he arrived on Tyneside, Newcastle were struggling and the Welsh international was assigned to a striker's role, his creative talents being largely wasted. The result was relegation to the Second Division and in August 1962, Allchurch returned to South Wales to play for Cardiff City for a fee of £18,000.

His debut for the Bluebirds came in a 4-4 draw against his former club Newcastle United and after scoring 12 goals in 35 games in that 1962-63 season, he was the club's top-scorer for the next two campaigns. In 1963-64 he netted his first hat-trick for the club in a 3-3 draw at Sunderland and the following season scored a hat-trick in a 5-0 demolition of his first club, Swansea!

In May 1966, Allchurch played his 68th and last game for Wales in Chile, a record which stood for twenty years until Joey Jones overtook him.

Having moved back to Swansea, he found himself a member of the team which attracted the record gate to the Vetch Field. The FA Cup match against Arsenal in February 1968, which the Gunners won 1-0 was watched by 32,786. As this was his last FA Cup match, it is an interesting fact that he played his first and last games in the competition against Arsenal - though they were separated by eighteen years !

The Queen presented him with the MBE for his services to Welsh football and in 1967-68, his last season of League football, he netted his seventh and final hat-trick for the Swans against Doncaster Rovers. Remarkably the then 38-year-old ended the campaign as the club's leading scorer with 21 League and Cup goals.

After leaving Swansea, he played non-League football for Worcester City, Haverfordwest and Pontardawe, turning out until past his fiftieth birthday before finally hanging up his boots.

WALLEY BARNES

Birthplace	Brecon
Born	16 January 1920
Died	10 September 1975

Football League Career

	Appearances	Goals
Arsenal	267	11

22 caps - 1 goal
(Arsenal)
1948 : v England, Scotland, N.Ireland
1949 : v England, Scotland, N.Ireland
1950 : v England, Scotland, N.Ireland, Belgium
1951 : v England, Scotland, N.Ireland, Portugal
1952 : v England, Scotland, N.Ireland, Rest of UK
1954 : v England, Scotland
1955 : v Scotland, Yugoslavia

One of the greatest full-backs that Arsenal have ever had, Walley Barnes was spotted while playing as an amateur inside-forward for Southampton, having earlier played for the Saints' south coast rivals, Portsmouth.

Arsenal signed him in the summer of 1943 and during the war years he played in every position except centre-forward, including a match in goal against Brighton which the Gunners won 3-1. At the end of the war, Barnes, who served as a sergeant major in the Army Physical Training Corps damaged his knee in a PT display and it was thought his career was over.

However, with guts and determination he worked his way back to full fitness and on 9 November 1946 he made his Football League debut for the Gunners in a 2-0 defeat at Preston North End. He was, at this stage of his career, 26 years old. Almost immediately the popular full-back won a regular place in Arsenal's League side and in 1947-48 won a Championship medal as well as the first of 22 Welsh caps when he played against England at Ninian Park. Following an injury to Laurie Scott, Barnes switched from playing left-back to right-back.

During 1949-50, Barnes became the club's regular penalty-taker, scoring his first in a 2-1 win at West Bromwich Albion. That season saw Barnes captain Wales for the first time as well as winning an FA Cup winners' medal as Arsenal beat Liverpool 2-0. In 1951-52, he missed only one League game as the Gunners finished third in the First Division and played a big part in helping the club reach the FA Cup Final where they met Newcastle United.

In the 33rd minute of this match, Walley Barnes tore his knee ligaments when he caught his studs in the Wembley turf and twisted his leg. Though the ten-men Arsenal side battled gamely, the Magpies won 1-0, courtesy of a George Robledo goal.

The injury kept Barnes out of action for the entire 1952-53 season but after working hard to regain full fitness, he returned to the Arsenal side for the visit of Chelsea to Highbury in September 1953. That season, Barnes scored his last penalty for the club - the winner in a 3-2 defeat of Preston North End, the club against whom Barnes had made his league debut. His knee problems though were to persist and in September 1955, he eventually gave up his struggle, asking for his contract to be cancelled.

Barnes, who was appointed Wales team manager in May 1954,. resigned from his post in October 1956 to become the BBC football adviser. He served the BBC in many capacities up to his untimely death at the age of fifty-five in September 1975.

Luton Town and coaching Kenton, he worked as a stock controller for a stationary concern in Wealdstone and was then employed as a warehouseman in South Harrow.

In 1964, Burgess had unsuccessfully applied for the vacant position of Wales team boss but he did assume control of the national side for a World Cup qualifying match against USSR in October 1965 when Dave Bowen was absent because of a League commitment. For the record, Wales won 2-1.

JOHN CHARLES

Birthplace   Cwmbwrla, Swansea
Born   27 December 1931

Football League Career

	Appearances	Goals
Leeds United	308	153
Cardiff City	65(1)	19

38 caps - 15 goals
(Leeds United)
1950 : v N.Ireland
1951 : v Switzerland
1953 : v N.Ireland France, Yugoslavia
1954 : v England, Scotland, N.Ireland, Austria
1955 : v Yugoslavia, Scotland, England, N.Ireland
1956 : v England Scotland, Austria, N.Ireland
1957 : v Scotland, England, N.Ireland, Czechoslovakia(2) E.Germany
         (Juventus)
1958: v Israel(2) Hungary(2) Mexico, Sweden
1960 : v Scotland

(Roma)
1962 : v England, Brazil(2) Mexico

(Leeds United)
1963 : v Scotland

(Cardiff City)
1964 : v Scotland
1965 : v Scotland, USSR

Few would argue with the description of John Charles as the greatest Welsh player of all time. Many Welshmen would go further and describe 'the gentle giant' as the greatest player of all time.

On leaving school in 1946, he joined the Swansea ground staff and soon began to show ability beyond that of his fellow apprentices. However, his stay at Vetch Field was brief. His talent was quickly spotted by Leeds United manager Major Frank Buckley and still an amateur, Charles was persuaded to go to Elland Road.

In January 1949 he signed professional forms and three months later, he made his League debut against Blackburn Rovers at centre-half. The following season he did not miss a League game and on 8 March 1950 he made his debut for Wales against Northern Ireland at Wrexham to become the youngest Welshman ever to represent his country. He was 18 years and 71 days old.

At 6ft 1 ins and 13 stone 12 lbs, Charles was as solid as a rock at the heart of the Leeds defence, yet he never used his immense body to stop opponents by foul means. However, he did come to blows in the army, fighting eleven boxing bouts during his National Service at Catterick before he was banned by the Amateur Boxing Association because he was a professional footballer. As the Yorkshire side bid for more goal power in an effort to climb out of Division Two, Charles was switched to centre-forward with devastating effect.

In 1953-54, Charles scored 42 goals to become the first Welshman to top the Football League scoring list, establishing a club record which is unlikely to be beaten. Only a leaky defence prevented promotion, so Charles temporarily returned to the back line to plug the gap, although he was later restored to the attack and netted 29 goals in the promotion season of 1955-56. In Division One, Charles continued to score with

John Charles

great regularity and Leeds were tagged 'Charles United' !

On 19 April 1957, he was chosen as captain of Wales for the first time and led them in a goalless draw against Northern Ireland in Belfast. But this was a milestone in Charles' career, for in the crowd was Umberto Agnelli, wealthy president of Juventus and so began one of the most talked about of all transfers.

Juventus were, at the time, struggling near the bottom of the Italian First Division. They needed players and with Agnelli of Fiat in charge, the money was there. For footballers in England, the money was most certainly not there. It was four years before the lifting of the maximum wage restriction and Charles was to start a minor emigration of star footballers from Britain to Italy. Within a week of the Belfast international, Leeds and Agnelli had agreed terms. It took Charles a little longer, months of negotiation in fact. But he signed in August in time for the Italian season and for the sort of money English footballers only dreamed about up to that time. It was all cloak and dagger stuff with Kenneth Wolstenholme and Terry Sommerfield representing Charles and negotiating between Sam Bolton, Percy Wood and Raich Carter of Leeds and Agnelli and his agent Gigi Peronace for Juventus.

The cost to Juventus was £65,000, a record fee for a British player. Within a year, a poll by the Italian football paper 'Il Calcio Illustrata' elected Charles the best player in the country.

Charles enjoyed the limelight. He bought a share in a restaurant, acquired a villa on the Italian Riviera as well as one in Turin.

Helped by Charles' 28 goals, Juventus won the Championship that year and two years later won both the Championship and Cup.

In the 1958 World Cup in Sweden, Charles was at centre-forward in the Wales team that drew with Hungary, Mexico and Sweden before beating Hungary in a play-off for the quarter-finals. Sadly, the savage treatment he had received ruled him out of the match against Brazil, the eventual winners. In all, Charles collected 38 caps for his country and could have had far more had he been available.

After five successful years, he decided to return to these shores, a decision he later regretted. Life at Elland Road under Don Revie's management was very different and in November 1962, after just three months at

Elland Road, he returned to Italy and Roma.

At Roma he began well, scoring within fifteen minutes of his first home match against Bologna, the League leaders. But injuries and a loss of form limited his appearances for Roma and he was dropped by Wales. Charles finally signed for Cardiff City for £20,000 at the end of that season.

But by now, Charles had slowed down and he reverted to a defender's role at Ninian Park. In 1966 he was transferred to non-League Hereford United for whom he scored 130 goals in 243 appearances. He left Hereford in September 1971, a year before the club attained their ambition of Football League status. After a spell as manager of Merthyr Tydfil, Charles became youth coach at Swansea in 1973 but left soccer three years later to become a publican in Leeds.

Charles now looks after the toy department of the children's shop which he and his wife run.

MEL CHARLES

Birthplace   Cwmbwrla, Swansea
Born   14 May 1935

Football League Career

	Appearances	Goals
Swansea City	233	69
Arsenal	60	26
Cardiff City	81	24
Port Vale	7	0

31 caps - 6 goals
(Swansea Town)
1955 : v N.Ireland
1956 : v England, Scotland, Austria
1957 : v England, N.Ireland, Czechoslovakia(2), E.Germany
1958 : v E.Germany, England, Scotland, Israel(2), Hungary(2), Mexico, Sweden, Brazil

1959 : v Scotland, England

(Arsenal)
1960 : v N.Ireland, Spain(2), Hungary
1962 : v England, Scotland, N.Ireland (Cardiff City) v Brazil
1963 : v Scotland, Hungary

Mel Charles showed early promise when he played for the Swansea Schools team which won the ESFA Trophy in 1950. After a trial with Leeds United, he signed professional forms for Swansea Town in May 1952.

Over the next seven seasons, Charles played in 233 League games for the Vetch Field club, scoring 69 goals. Also whilst with the Swans, he won 21 Welsh caps, including playing in the 1958 World Cup Finals in Sweden when he was voted the best centre-half in the tournament. He had made his international debut in April 1955 when he played right-half in a 3-2 win over Northern Ireland in Belfast and showed his versatility by scoring all four goals against the same opposition seven years later when Wales won 4-0 at Ninian Park.

Like his brother John, he became very much sought after and in March 1959 he joined Arsenal for a Highbury club record fee of £42,750 plus Gunners' youngsters Peter Davies and David Dodson. Charles was seen as the player around whom manager George Swindin could build a title-winning side. He made his First Division debut for the Gunners at centre-half against Sheffield Wednesday in August 1959 and went on to appear in twenty league games, alternating between centre-half and centre-forward. Sadly, the multi-gifted Welshman's Highbury career was devastated by two cartilage operations and in his first two seasons with the club, he started less than half the Gunners' games. Even when he did turn out, he often played carrying injuries. He started the 1961-62 season as the club's first-choice centre-forward and scored two goals against Everton and a hat-trick in the defeat of Blackburn Rovers. Majestic in the air and possessing intricate skills for such a big man, he netted 17 goals in 23 League and Cup games that season before returning to Wales to sign for Cardiff City for £28,500 in February 1962.

For the Bluebirds he scored 24 goals in 81 League games and took his total of international appearances to 31 before being displaced by brother John on his return from Italy.

He then played non-League football for Porthmadog in the Welsh League (North) before returning to League action with Port Vale at the end of the 1966-67 season. He later played for Haverfordwest before hanging up his boots.

On retirement he went into business in his home-town of Swansea before becoming involved in the Swansea Council scheme of sport for the unemployed. Along with his brother John, he guided the fortunes of his son Jeremy, who played League football for Swansea City, Queen's Park Rangers and Oxford United as well as winning 19 caps for Wales.

ROY CLARKE

Birthplace   Crindau, Newport
Born   1 June 1925

Football League Career

	Appearances	Goals
Cardiff City	39	11
Manchester City	349	73
Stockport County	25	5

22 caps - 5 goals
(Manchester City)
1949 : v England 1949
1950 : v Scotland, Belgium, N.Ireland
1951 : v Scotland, England, N.Ireland, Portugal, Switzerland
1952 : v England, Scotland, Rest of the UK
1953 : v N.Ireland, Scotland, England
1954 : v England, Scotland, N.Ireland
1955 : v Yugoslavia, Scotland, England
1956 : v N.Ireland

Roy Clarke's first taste of international recognition was as a member of the Welsh Schools Baseball team in 1939. During the Second World War he worked in the coalmines but managed to play for local side Albion Rovers of Newport at the weekends.

Cardiff City won the race for his signature in 1942 and his early performances on the left-wing were impressive enough to earn him a place in the Wales team for the Victory International of 1946 against Northern Ireland. As it turned out, Clarke played less than one full season of peacetime football for the Bluebirds, his speedy hard-shooting forays down the left flank being a feature of a Cardiff side that won promotion to the Second Division in 1946-47.

Towards the end of that season, Manchester City paid £12,000 for Clarke's services.

Roy Clarke holds the unique record of playing in three different divisions of the Football League in three consecutive league games ! He played the last of his 39 games for the Bluebirds in the penultimate game of the 1946-47 season before he joined the Maine Road club. He played in Manchester City's last game of their Second Division promotion-winning season against his home-town club, Newport County - a game in which George Smith scored all five goals as City beat the Welsh side 5-1. Clarke's next game was at the start of the 1947-48 campaign with the Maine Road club in the top flight. They beat Wolves 4-3 at Molineux with Roy Clarke hitting the winner.

Clarke returned to Ninian Park in 1949 to win the first of 22 Welsh caps in a World Cup qualifying game against England which was lost 4-1. His last came some seven years later against Northern Ireland, a 1-1 draw at the same venue.

Plying his trade down the left-wing, Roy Clarke provided many chances for the likes of Broadis, Westcott and Williamson as well as cutting in himself to score a number of vital goals during his stay at Maine Road.

Clarke was instrumental in City getting to Wembley at the end of the 1954-55 campaign. He hit both goals in the 2-0 win at Kenilworth Road as City disposed of Luton Town in the fifth round. He also hit the only goal of the semi-final against Sunderland at Villa Park but unfortunately he missed the final against Newcastle United because of injury.

Roy Clarke

The following season though he picked up an FA Cup winners' medal after City had beaten Birmingham 3-1. Clarke's best season for the Maine Road club in terms of goals scored was 1956-57 when he scored 11 goals from his 40 appearances.

After the arrival of Ray Sambrook from Coventry City to contest the Number 11 shirt along with Paddy Fagan and Clarke, he moved on to Stockport County on a free transfer as recognition of his sterling service. Clarke held the post of player-coach and then caretaker-manager. On leaving Edgeley Park, he played non-League football for Northwich Victoria and Whalley Range before hanging up his boots.

He returned to Maine Road in 1966 to run the City Social Club. After twenty-two years, he retired on 27 September 1988, with hundreds of friends and colleagues paying tribute to him in a farewell party at Maine Road.

ALAN CURTIS

Birthplace	Rhondda
Born	16 April 1954

Football League Career

	Appearances	Goals
Swansea City	347(17)	96
Leeds United	28	5
Southampton	43(7)	5
Stoke City	3	0
Cardiff City	122(3)	10

35 caps - 6 goals
(Swansea City)
1976 : v England(2) Yugoslavia(2) Scotland, N.Ireland
1977 : v W.Germany, Scotland, N.Ireland
1978 : v W.Germany, England, Scotland
1979 : v W.Germany, Scotland

(Leeds United)
1979 : v England, N.Ireland, Malta
1980 : v Eire, W.Germany, Turkey

(Swansea City)
1982 : v Czechoslovakia, Iceland, USSR, Spain, England, Scotland, N.Ireland
1983 : v Norway
1984 : v Romania

(Southampton)
1984 : v Scotland
1985 : v Spain, Norway(2)
1986 : v Hungary

(Cardiff City)
1987: v USSR

A nephew of former Swansea, Manchester City and Welsh international Roy Paul, Alan Curtis had been taken onto the Swansea groundstaff directly from school and soon emerged as a first team player of skill, vision and imagination. He made his first team debut for the Swans against Charlton Athletic in the final game of the 1972-73 season. Curtis became quite a prolific marksman, netting his first first-team hat-trick in a 4-1 Welsh Cup win over Newport County in January 1977 and ended the season with 14 goals. His first League hat-trick came in a 5-0 win over Crewe Alexandra in November 1977, whilst five months later both Curtis and Robbie James scored hat-tricks as the Swans recorded their biggest-ever League win, defeating Hartlepool United 8-0.

Curtis built his reputation as Swansea surged out of the lower reaches of the League and in May 1979 he joined Leeds United for £400,000, a record for a player from the lower divisions. Curtis arrived at Elland Road in triumphant form, scoring two goals on his debut in a 2-2 draw against Bristol City. Though injury and a loss of form restricted his career with the Yorkshire club to eighteen months, he did provide a handful of memorable moments. In October 1979, Leeds, who had endured six months without an away win, travelled to Southampton. It was here that Curtis scored a glorious individual goal, when in the dying seconds of the game, he ran almost the full length of the pitch to drive home a long-range shot that provided Leeds with a 2-1 victory.

Curtis returned to the Vetch Field in December 1980 as the Swans paid £165,000 to take him back to South Wales. In his first game with the Swans in his second spell, he scored the only goal of the game from the penalty-spot against Watford. He went on to be an important member of the Swansea side that won promotion to the First Division for the first time in the club's history.

A regular for Wales, Curtis left the Vetch Field for a second time in November 1983, following the club's relegation from the top flight. He joined Southampton for £85,000, to ease the Swan's financial plight. At the Dell, he failed to show his best form and in March 1986 he was loaned

Alan Curtis

to Stoke City. Things didn't work out for him at the Victoria Ground and he returned to South Wales again to play for Cardiff City, whom he joined on a free transfer.

In 1987-88, Curtis was instrumental in the club winning promotion to the Third Division and the Welsh Cup, in which he scored one of the goals in a 2-0 win over Wrexham. In the final game of that season, a 2-2 draw at Burnley, in which Curtis scored one of Cardiff's goals, he notched up his 500th League appearance. He continued to be a regular member of the Bluebirds' first team in 1988-89 but during the early part of the following season, he returned to the Vetch Field for a third spell. He announced his retirement at the end of the 1989-90 season, after having scored 96 goals in 364 league games for the Swans. He then joined Barry Town as player-coach in the summer of 1990 before signing for Haverfordwest County in July 1991.

After a spell working as a financial consultant for a life insurance company, he is now back at Vetch Field as assistant-manager to John Hollins.

RAY DANIEL

Birthplace   Swansea
Born   2 November 1928

Football League Career

	Appearances	Goals
Arsenal	87	5
Sunderland	136	6
Cardiff City	6	0
Swansea City	45	7

21 caps:
(Arsenal)
1951 : v England, N.Ireland, Portugal
1952 : v England, Scotland, N.Ireland, Rest of the UK
1953 : v Scotland, England, N.Ireland, France, Yugoslavia

(Sunderland)
1954 : v England, Scotland, N.Ireland
1955 : v England, N.Ireland
1957 : v Scotland, England, N.Ireland, Czechoslovakia

Though he attended the same school as the young Ivor Allchurch, it was Ray's brother Bobby, who was very much the local soccer starlet. He not only captained Swansea Schools but won Welsh Schoolboy international honours in 1938. Sadly, just after he had been signed by Arsenal, Bobby was killed on active service whilst serving with the RAF. This terrible tragedy spurred Ray on to consider a career in the game and during the latter stages of the Second World War, he played as an amateur for Swansea.

In October 1946 he too was offered a chance at Highbury and signed for the Gunners without any hesitation. His early days with the North London club were spent in the reserves at Hendon, being groomed as a successor to the club's ageing first team centre-half Leslie Compton. Called up for National Service in January 1947, he returned to Highbury and made his League debut against Charlton Athletic on 7 May 1949, as Compton ended the season early to play cricket for Middlesex. Daniel's first five seasons at Highbury were spent in the club's reserve side, it being 1951-52 before he made the position his own.

The Welsh selectors had no qualms about picking him, even though he wasn't a regular in the Arsenal side. He won his first full cap in November 1950 when he gave an impressive display against Jackie Milburn in a 4-2 defeat by England at Roker Park. Daniel went on to win 21 caps for Wales, building up a fine understanding with Ron Burgess and Roy Paul. Though he was later displaced by John Charles, the flamboyant defender won his place back in the side when Charles moved to play centre-forward.

Though he had broken a wrist, which was set in plaster, Daniel passed a late fitness test to line-up in the Arsenal side to play Newcastle United in the 1952 FA Cup Final. Early in the game, Daniel clashed with Milburn, the Magpies' centre-forward and the partly-knitted bone was broken again. Though he battled on bravely, the Gunners lost 1-0. Daniel was a regular in the Arsenal side again the following season, missing only one match as

29

the Highbury club won the League Championship on goal difference from Preston North End. It was thought that Daniel would be the next Arsenal captain but after yet another disagreement with manager Tom Whittaker, he was allowed to leave Highbury in the summer of 1953, joining Sunderland for a record £30,000.

Teaming up with fellow Welsh international Trevor Ford, he made his debut for the Wearsiders against Charlton Athletic at The Valley on the opening day of the 1953-54 season, a game which Sunderland lost 5-3. Over the next four seasons, Daniel was a virtual ever-present in the Sunderland side, though by and large, he, along with the other great individuals such as Billy Bingham, Trevor Ford and Len Shackleton failed to blend as a team. During his time at Roker Park, allegations regarding illegal bonuses paid to a number of players were reported to the Football League and Daniel was one of those suspended. Sadly, it not only cost him a fine but but also restricted his appearances for Wales.

His last game for his country came in May 1957 when he was rushed to Czechoslovakia to play in a World Cup game, just a matter of days after the suspension had been lifted.

Daniel later had a short spell with Cardiff City before ending his League career with his home-town club, Swansea. After playing part-time non-League football for Hereford United, he worked as an area manager for Courvoisier Brandy but is now postmaster at Cockett Post Office.

DAI DAVIES

Birthplace	Ammanford
Born	1 April 1948

Football League Career

	Appearances	Goals
Swansea City	86	0
Everton	82	0
Wrexham	144	0
Tranmere Rovers	42	0

52 caps:
(Everton)
1975 : v Hungary, Luxembourg, Scotland, England, N.Ireland
1976 : v Yugoslavia(2) England, N.Ireland
1977 : v W.Germany, Scotland(2) Czechoslovakia, England, N.Ireland
1978 : v Kuwait 1978

(Wrexham)
1978 : v Scotland(2) Czechoslovakia, W.Germany, Iran, England,
    N.Ireland
1979 : v Malta(2) Turkey, W.Germany, Scotland, England, N.Ireland
1980 : v Eire, W.Germany, Turkey, England, Scotland, N.Ireland, Iceland
1981 : v Turkey(2) Czechoslovakia, Eire, Scotland, England, USSR

(Swansea City)
1982 : v Czechoslovakia, Iceland, USSR, Spain, England, Scotland,
    France
1983 : v Yugoslavia

Born in the South Wales mining village of Ammanford, goalkeeper Dai Davies tasted early success with Cardiff College of Education in 1969 when they won the Welsh Amateur Cup.

He began his Football League career with Swansea City, making his debut for the Vetch Field club against Third Division champions Chesterfield in the final game of the 1969-70 season. His first game in 1970-71 was against Preston North End, a match the Welsh side drew 1-1 before going on to complete a remarkable sequence of 19 matches undefeated, to equal the club record set some ten years earlier.

In December 1970, Davies signed for Everton for £25,000 but after spending virtually four seasons in the shadow of Gordon West and his understudy David Lawson, he went back to the Vetch Field on loan. Eventually he returned to Goodison Park and went on to appear in 94 League and Cup games before leaving to join Wrexham in September 1977 for £8,000. Whilst with Everton, he gained the first of 52 Welsh caps when he played in Wales' 2-1 win over Hungary in Budapest.

Dai Davies

In his first season at the Racecourse Ground, Wrexham suffered the lowest number of defeats in their history as they won the Third Division Championship. In 1978-79 the Wrexham 'keeper helped establish the club's best-ever defensive record of only 42 goals conceded. The Robins won the Welsh Cup and qualified for Europe. At the beginning of that season, the Welsh-speaking Davies was accorded a rare honour when he became the first soccer player to be admitted to the Gorsedd circle at the Cardiff National Eisteddfod. He chose the bardic name 'Dai o'r cwm' - Dai of the Valleys, after his native Amman valley.

At the end of the 1980-81 season, he returned to play for Swansea where he was unbeaten in six consecutive matches.

In the summer of 1983, Davies joined Tranmere Rovers as the Prenton Park club's player-coach. A year later he retired from the game but in 1985, Bangor City qualified for Europe and Davies came out of retirement to play in the European Cup Winners' Cup matches against Fredrikstad and Atletico Madrid. The following season he turned out in Wrexham's Welsh Cup campaign, winning a medal after Kidderminster Harriers were beaten in the final.

Davies was a commanding goalkeeper who dominated his penalty area and though he was prone to the odd mistake, he was a permanent fixture in the Welsh side, keeping his place for some eight years. When he turned out against Scotland at Swansea in 1981, Davies overtook Jack Kelsey's record of 41 caps, going on to concede just fifty-one goals in fifty-two games, the best record of all modern Welsh goalkeepers.

He became involved in a Welsh book and craft shop in Mold and could be heard commenting on football on Welsh TV. Although a qualified teacher, Davies now runs a natural healing centre in Llangollen, North Wales.

RON DAVIES

Birthplace   Holywell
Born   25 May 1942

Football League Career

	Appearances	Goals
Chester City	94	44
Luton Town	32	21
Norwich City	113	58
Southampton	239(1)	134
Portsmouth	59	18
Manchester United	0(8)	0
Millwall	3	0

29 caps - 9 goals
(Norwich.C)
1964 : v N.Ireland
1965 : v England
1966 : v Brazil(2) Chile

(Southampton)
1967 : v Scotland, England, N.Ireland
1968 : v Scotland, N.Ireland, W.Germany
1969 : v Italy, W.Germany, Scotland, England, N.Ireland
1970 : v Rest of the UK, England, Scotland, N.Ireland
1971 : v Czechoslovakia, Scotland, England, N.Ireland
1972 : v Romania, England, Scotland, N.Ireland

(Portsmouth)
1974 : v England

Ron Davies was one of the most consistent post-war goalscorers and there was a time when his heading ability made him probably the most sought after player in the top flight.

He was at school with Mike England who completely overshadowed the young Davies and was taken on as an apprentice by Blackburn Rovers. Davies though was determined to succeed and he trained by hurdling in Army boots to build up his strength and leaping powers. Eventually spotted by John Harris, then the Chester manager, he began to train with other schoolboys, making the journey from Holywell to Chester by bus twice a week. On leaving school, he began to work in the local steelworks as an apprentice moulder but after five weeks, Davies was employed as a groundstaff boy, the first Chester had ever had. Still only 17, he won a place in the side towards the end of the 1959-60 season, playing in eight games and scoring one goal. The following season he gained a regular place in the Chester side that finished bottom of the Fourth Division, scoring 23 goals in 39 appearances, the sixth highest scorer in the division. In the last game of the season at Hartlepool United, Chester needed to win to the avoid the humiliation of being bottom of the League. Davies helped his side score four times, grabbing two fine goals himself but his defence let in four, so Chester were last !

He topped the club's goalscoring charts again the following season but at the beginning of the 1961-62 campaign, he was surprisingly dropped. Aggrieved, he asked for a transfer and was put on offer at £3,000. He then got back in the side, scored four goals in a 6-1 win over Southport and when he joined Luton Town a few weeks later, his transfer value had soared to £10,000.

Though the Hatters were relegated to the Third Division in Davies' first season at Kenilworth Road, he more than repaid his transfer fee, having scored 21 goals in 29 games for his new club.

In September 1963, Davies joined Norwich City for a record transfer fee of £35,000. His first season at Carrow Road brought him 27 goals as he revelled in the service he was given from two wingers whose task it was to find Davies' blond head ! Over the next couple of seasons, Davies continued to score goals but Norwich were not winning anything and he became unhappy.

It seemed as if he would get his wish to play First Division football when Newcastle United manager Joe Harvey had him watched frequently and even contacted Norwich. However, he seemed reluctant to commit himself to an expensive player who had scored a lot of goals but none of them in the top flight.

Davies eventually left Carrow Road to play First Division football for Southampton in August 1966 when the Saints paid a record £55,000 to take him to the Dell. Davies was already an established Welsh international, scoring on his debut in a 4-1 win against Northern Ireland at Wrexham in 1963.

Southampton were about to embark on their first season in Division One but even the most optimistic of Saints' fans did not expect Davies to make the impact he did. In 1966-67 he scored 38 First Division goals to become the Football League's top marksman - five further efforts in cup-ties made him the leading goalscorer in Europe. With crosses from Paine and Sydenham floating in, Davies continued to dominate the aerial battles and in 1967-68 he scored another 28 goals to retain his title as the Football League's leading scorer - sharing the honour with Manchester United's George Best.

His success at the Dell turned him into a new commodity for his country. In May 1969 he really established himself as a striker of true international worth with three spectacular headers in the Home International Tournament.

Davies' heading powers were awesome and when in August 1969 he scored four goals at Old Trafford, Matt Busby said that Davies had no peer in Europe. In fact, United headed a whole host of top clubs who were willing to pay a small fortune for Davies' services but Southampton were determined to hold on to him.

By 1973 he was suffering from a series of injuries sustained from too many robust tackles and could no longer command a regular first team place. Portsmouth signed him that April and in 59 games for Saints' main rivals, he scored 18 goals. Manchester United had not forgotten Davies and they surprised the football world by signing him in November 1974. He never began a game in United's first team but made eight substitute appearances before joining Millwall for three League games in November 1975.

After hanging up his boots, Davies used his penmanship and cartoonist skills to forge another successful career on the south coast before moving to California in 1985 where he coached college youngsters. Now living in Florida, he coaches Orlando Lions, as well as giving private tuition to football crazy kids!

Ron Davies

Wyn Davies

up well and controlled the forward line. Very much a provider of chances, the target man up front, he was never lethal in front of goal, though he did grab his share of goals, mostly with powerful headers that found the back of the net. As the Magpies surged into European competition, Davies became one of the most feared strikers on the continent, scoring 10 goals in 24 games and helping the club win the Inter Cities Fairs Cup in 1969. However, once the club had been eliminated from Europe in 1970, Newcastle manager Joe Harvey decided to dispense with Davies' style of play and following an injury he found it difficult to get back into the side. During the summer of 1971, Davies left the north-east to return to Lancashire to team up with his long-standing admirer Joe Mercer at Manchester City.

He remained only briefly at Maine Road before moving across Manchester to Old Trafford. Playing in a struggling team and alongside another non-established striker in Ted MacDougall, any hope he had of an Indian summer disappeared with the appointment of Tommy Docherty as manager. After a short spell with Blackpool, he headed south for an equally brief stint with Crystal Palace. Stockport County signed him in August 1975 before he ended his long career with Crewe Alexandra.

He retired from senior football in 1978 but continued playing with Northern Premier League side, Bangor City and also in South Africa's National Football League for Pretoria club, Arcadia Shepherds. He later returned to England and settled in Bolton, working as a baker, though he still holds on to the dream that one day he will own a smallholding in his native Caernarfon.

ALAN DURBAN

Birthplace   Port Talbot
Born   7 July 1941

Football League Career

	Appearances	Goals
Cardiff City	52	9
Derby County	336(10)	93
Shrewsbury Town	150(6)	33

27 caps: 2 goals
(Derby.C)
1966: v Brazil
1967: v N.Ireland
1968: v England, Scotland, N.Ireland; W.Germany
1969: v W.Germany; E.Germany; Scotland; England; N.Ireland
1970: v E.Germany; Italy; England; Scotland; N.Ireland
1971: v Romania; Czechoslovakia; Scotland; England; N.Ireland; Finland
1972: v Finland; Czechoslovakia; England; Scotland; N.Ireland

Though he could quite easily have made the grade at cricket, lawn tennis or rugby union, by the time Alan Durban left Port Talbot Grammar School, a number of soccer scouts were competing for his signature.

Durban joined Cardiff City in September 1958 and made his league debut a year later in a 2-1 win at Derby County, the club with which he was to make his name. After an in-and-out period at Ninian Park, Durban was transferred to Derby County where manager Tim Ward paid £10,000 for his services. It was certainly money well spent, for Durban was one of the few players at the Baseball Ground to survive and play a significant role in the Brian Clough era.

Durban had two distinct phases at Derby County, the first as a goalscoring inside-forward and the second as an intelligent midfield player. In his first role, he scored 24 goals in 1964-65, a total equalled by his partner Eddie Thomas, who had joined the Rams from Swansea Town. Durban went on to score 112 goals in 403 first team outings for Derby including four hat-tricks but there is no doubt that his best days at the club were when he played in midfield.

Though he lacked pace and wasn't a particularly good tackler, he had a great first touch and a wonderful feel for the flow of the game. Perhaps his greatest attribute was his ability to find space in crowded penalty areas, often arriving late to score a large number of his goals from close range.

Durban spent ten years at the Baseball Ground and was a major influence in the team's rise to the First Division and in 1971-72, the capture of the Football League Championship.

He earned 27 Welsh caps, his first against Brazil in 1966 before joining Shrewsbury Town in September 1973, later becoming player-manager. He steered the club out of the Fourth Division in 1974-75 and to Welsh Cup success. When he hung up his boots, Durban had played in more than 550 League games and appeared at all 92 grounds !

In February 1978, Durban was appointed manager of Stoke City. Here he introduced more discipline into the club and appointed Howard Kendall as his chief coach. The Potters won promotion to the First Division in 1978-79 and though he made quite a few new signings in the close season, Stoke struggled to avoid relegation from the top flight the following season.

He left for Sunderland after a more tempting offer, taking on the enormous task of restoring the Wearsiders to some of their former greatness. However, after three troubled years in which the club struggled in the relegation zone of the First Division, he was sacked. Six months later he moved back to his first club, Cardiff City as manager but it turned out to be a bad move. When the Bluebirds suffered relegation in two successive seasons, Durban was dismissed.

The only Welsh international soccer player to have competed in the All England tennis championships at Wimbledon, he became disillusioned with the game and left soccer to become manager of the Telford Indoor Tennis Centre.

MIKE ENGLAND

Birthplace   Holywell
Born   2 December 1941

Football League Career

	Appearances	Goals
Blackburn Rovers	165	21
Tottenham Hotspur	300	14
Cardiff City	40	1

44 caps: 4 goals.
1962: v (Blackburn.R) v N.Ireland, Brazil, Mexico
1963: v N.Ireland, Hungary,
1964: v England, Scotland, N.Ireland,
1965: v England, Denmark, Greece(2) USSR, N.Ireland, Italy
1966: v England, Scotland, N.Ireland, USSR, Denmark
1967: v (Tottenham.H) v Scotland, England
1968: v England, N.Ireland, W.Germany
1969: v E.Germany
1970: v Rest of UK, E.Germany, England, Scotland, N.Ireland, Italy
1971: v Romania
1972: v Finland, England, Scotland, N.Ireland,
1973: v England(3) Scotland
1974: v Poland
1975: v Hungary, Luxembourg

One of the few Welshmen to have both played and managed that country, Mike England began his career in the same Ysgol Dinas Basing school team as his future international team-mate Ron Davies. At the age of 15 he was offered the choice of joining Blackburn Rovers or Glamorgan County Cricket Club. He accepted the Ewood Park club's offer and was a member of Blackburn's FA Youth Cup winning side of 1959. He played for Rovers at outside-right, half-back and centre-forward before settling in central defence where he was soon acknowledged as the best young centre-half in the Football League. He had made his league debut as a 17-year-old against Preston North End during the 1959-60 season, giving a good account of himself against the likes of Tom Finney and Tommy Thompson.

England's versatility was used by his country at Under-23 level, when he was played at inside-forward as well as in the half-back line. He went on to play in a record 11 games at this level, many of his appearances coming after he had made his full international debut against Northern Ireland in April 1962, a match Wales won 4-0.

It was at the start of the 1963-64 season when England was installed as Blackburn's first-choice centre-half. His height made him dominant in the air, whilst on the ground, his strength and speed made him a daunting prospect for even the quickest of opposition forwards. However, England's game was not just based on power, his deft touches, instant control and accurate distribution put him into a class of his own. Gradually he began to become somewhat disenchanted with the Ewood Park club who, it seemed, lacked ambition in the top flight as they let a number of their better players join top clubs. However, Rovers initially refused to allow him to try his luck with a bigger club and so England, who was a stubborn and fiercely ambitious player, threatened to quit the game altogether. After a series of transfer requests, Rovers, for whom England had scored 21 goals in 184 League and Cup games, finally relented and sold him to Tottenham Hotspur in August 1966.

The fee of £95,000 was a British record for a defender and it wasn't long before he became a great favourite with the White Hart Lane crowd. In his first season with Spurs he helped the club lift the FA Cup, giving a superb performance in the final to dominate Chelsea's Tony Hateley. Despite missing the 1971 League Cup Final with an ankle injury, he helped Spurs win the 1972 UEFA Cup and the 1973 League Cup. He also appeared and scored in the 1974 UEFA Cup Final and together with Pat Jennings, provided a solid core to the Spurs defence.

He did the same for Wales, captaining his country and taking his total of full international caps to 44.

In March 1975, aged 33, he was troubled by ankle problems and with Spurs struggling against relegation, he quite suddenly announced his

45

Mike England

retirement after scoring 20 goals in 434 games for the White Hart Lane club.

However, he re-emerged the following August to play for one season with Cardiff City, having spent the summer with Seattle Sounders. He helped the Bluebirds win promotion from the Third Division and then spent four further American summers playing for Seattle, appearing for Team America and in the 1976 Bi-Centennial Tournament with England, Brazil and Italy. It was while he was in America that he heard of the vacancy for the Welsh manager's position after Mike Smith had taken up a club appointment.

He was successful with his application and his first game in charge in May 1980 saw Wales beat England 4-1 at Wrexham. Despite the limited resources at his disposal, England took Wales close to qualification for both the World Cup and European Championships. During his time in charge of the national side, he helped to guide the international careers of Ian Rush, Mark Hughes, Neville Southall and Kevin Ratcliffe and in 1984 he was awarded the MBE for his services to Welsh soccer.

In February 1988, Mike England was controversially sacked after Wales had yet again just avoided qualification for a major championship. As with all major football decisions, opinions were divided on the wisdom of such a move. Though there were those who questioned his tactical approach, the majority recognised his great qualities as a motivator of players.

On leaving the game, England returned to live in North Wales where he is a businessman and owns residential homes in Rhyl and Colwyn Bay.

BRIAN FLYNN

Birthplace   Port Talbot
Born   12 October 1955

Football League Career

	Appearances	Goals
Burnley	193(8)	19
Leeds United	152(2)	11
Cardiff City	32	0
Doncaster Rovers	45(6)	1
Bury	19	0
Wrexham	91(9)	5

66 caps: 7 goals.
(Burnley)
1975: v Luxembourg(2) Hungary, Scotland, England, N.Ireland
1976: v Austria, England(2) Yugoslavia(2) N.Ireland
1977: v W.Germany, Scotland(2) Czechoslovakia, England, N.Ireland
1978: v Kuwait(2) Scotland (Leeds.U) v Czechoslovakia, W.Germany, Iran, England, Scotland, N.Ireland
1979: v Malta(2) Turkey, Scotland, England, N.Ireland
1980: v Eire, W.Germany, England, Scotland, N.Ireland, Iceland
1981: v Turkey(2) Czechoslovakia, Eire? Scotland, England, USSR
1982: v Czechoslovakia, USSR, England, Scotland, N.Ireland, France
1983: v Norway (Burnley) v Yugoslavia, England, Bulgaria, Scotland, N.Ireland, Brazil
1984: v Norway(2) Romania, Bulgaria, Yugoslavia, Scotland, Israel

A Welsh Schoolboy international, Brian Flynn was first spotted playing for Neath Boys by Cardiff City but the Ninian Park club let him slip through the net and in 1971, Burnley signed him as an apprentice. He turned professional the following year but had to wait until February 1974 before making his league debut for the Clarets in a First Division match at Arsenal. It was early the following season that the 5ft 3ins

Flynn began to establish himself in the Burnley midfield, his performances earning him a first Welsh cap at the age of 19 when he played against Luxembourg at Swansea in November 1974.

Flynn was not a prolific goalscorer and in fact scored for his country in his third international against Scotland in May 1975 before finding the net in a league match for Burnley, a feat he achieved in a 3-2 win at Everton in January 1976.

Following Burnley's relegation to the Second Division in 1975-76, it was always going to be difficult for the Turf Moor club to hold on to its stars. In November 1977, Flynn left the Clarets to join Leeds United for a fee of £175,000 and immediately forged a superb midfield partnership with England international Tony Currie.

Although the more flamboyant skills of Currie grabbed the headlines, it was Flynn's voracious appetite for work and his variety of defence-splitting passes that caught the eye. Flynn also had good control and a neat first touch and had a longer stay at Elland Road than his midfield partner but as Allan Clarke made fruitless experiments in an attempt to stave off relegation, Flynn returned to Burnley on loan in March 1982, eventually signing on a permanent basis at the end of the year. He took his tally of goals to 27 in 254 League and Cup games before leaving to play for Cardiff City in November 1984. After spells with Doncaster Rovers and Bury he teamed up with former Burnley and Northern Ireland international Billy Hamilton at Limerick in 1987 as the club's player-coach.

He then had another spell with Doncaster and then after working on the Football in the Community Scheme at Burnley, he joined Wrexham in February 1988.

When the Robins' manager Dixie McNeil resigned in the early part of the 1989-90 season, Flynn was asked to take over as player-manager of the Racecourse Ground club. After two disastrous campaigns and finishing bottom of the Fourth Division in 1990-91, Flynn began to turn things around and after Wrexham had beaten Arsenal, the reigning League Champions in the third round of the FA Cup, the football world began to take notice of the Robins. In 1992-93 he led the club to promotion to the new Second Division. Since then, the club have come close to the play-offs on a number of occasions, perhaps none more so than in 1997-98 when they finished seventh, as Flynn, a player who won 66 caps for Wales, demonstrated that he has the credentials to go to the top in football management.

Brian Flynn

TREVOR FORD

Birthplace   Swansea
Born   1 October 1923

Football League Career

	Appearances	Goals
Swansea City	16	9
Aston Villa	120	60
Sunderland	108	67
Cardiff City	96	39
Newport County	8	3

38 caps: 23 goals.
1947: (Swansea) v Scotland;(Aston Villa) v N.Ireland
1948: v Scotland, N.Ireland
1949: v Scotland, England, N.Ireland, Portugal, Belgium, Switzerland
1950: v England, Scotland, Belgium, N.Ireland
1951: v Scotland (Sunderland) v England, N.Ireland, Portugal, Switzerland
1952: v England, Scotland, Rest of UK, N.Ireland
1953: v Scotland, England, N.Ireland, France, Yugoslavia
1954: (Cardiff.C) v Austria
1955: v Yugoslavia, Scotland, England, N.Ireland
1956: v England, Scotland, Austria, N.Ireland
1957: v Scotland

Trevor Ford was one of the leading forwards of his day, though as a schoolboy he played for the Swansea team as a full-back, only missing Welsh Schoolboy honours due to a broken leg.

During the Second World War, Ford served in the Royal Artillery and with the unit team short of a centre-forward, his sergeant-major decided to try him up front. Having signed for his home-town club in 1942, Ford graduated into the Swans' first team during the latter stages of the hostilities. In 1945-46 he scored 44 goals in 41 games for Swansea and gained a place in the Welsh side for the last Victory international of the season against Northern Ireland at Ninian Park. Despite a disappointing debut, Ford kept his place in the side for the opening international of the following season and scored his first goal for his country in a 3-1 win over Scotland at Wrexham.

Not surprisingly, a number of First Division clubs began to show an interest in Trevor Ford and after scoring nine goals in the opening six games of the 1946-47 season, he joined Aston Villa for a fee of £12,000.

He made his Villa debut in a 2-0 win at Highbury in January 1947 and in nine games that season, scored nine goals. In terms of goals scored, his best seasons were 1947-48 and 1949-50 when he netted 18 in each campaign, although on 27 December 1948, he scored four goals as Villa beat Wolverhampton Wanderers 5-1.

Whilst with Villa, Ford received offers to go and play in Colombia whose sides were out of the jurisdiction of FIFA and so were able to pay much higher wages. He was definitely interested but when Welsh teammate Roy Paul returned dissatisfied from a trip to South America, he decided against a move. Ford received another offer from a Portuguese club whilst on international duty in Lisbon but again rejected the overture.

However, in October 1950, Ford left Villa Park after scoring 61 goals in 128 games and signed for Sunderland for £30,000.

After playing his first game in Sunderland colours in a 3-0 defeat at Chelsea, he scored a hat-trick on his home debut when Sheffield Wednesday were beaten 5-1. He top-scored for the Wearsiders over the next two seasons, netting a hat-trick in a 4-1 home win over Chelsea in February 1952 and four goals in a 5-2 defeat of Manchester City at Maine Road in November 1952. He netted another hat-trick at the start of the 1953-54 campaign when Arsenal were beaten 4-1 but a few weeks later, after scoring 70 goals in 117 League and Cup games, he joined Cardiff City for what was then the Bluebirds' record fee of £30,000.

For Wales, Ford soon became the leading goalscorer of all-time, netting a hat-trick in a 5-1 win over Belgium and two goals against England at Wembley in 1952. By the time he played the last of his 38 internationals against Scotland in 1957, he had a record 23 goals to his credit.

Ford soon became a firm favourite with the Cardiff supporters and though not as prolific a scorer as in his early playing days, he did net four goals in two Welsh Cup games as Pembroke Borough were beaten 7-0 in 1954-55 and 9-0 in 1955-56. He had scored 59 goals in 119 outings for the Bluebirds when in 1955 he fell out with Trevor Morris following the City manager's decision to play him at inside-right.

After leaving Ninian Park, Ford was banned *sine die* by the Football League following his revelations about Sunderland Football Club in his autobiography 'I lead the attack' which was serialised in a Sunday newspaper. Though he was later reinstated he was banned again when Football League Secretary Alan Hardaker uncovered an illegal payment of £100 by Sunderland to Ford.

He went abroad and spent three successful years in Holland with PSV Eindhoven where in 1957-58 he scored a remarkable 51 goals. He returned to these shores after the suspension was lifted to play for Newport County and later non-League Romford but sadly a knee injury curtailed his playing career. While he had been at Sunderland, Ford had entered the motor trade and on returning to South Wales, pursued this career.

RYAN GIGGS

Birthplace   Cardiff
Born   29 November 1973

Football League Career

	Appearances	Goals
Manchester United	237(23)	53

24 caps: 5 goals.
1992: (Manchester.U) v Germany, Luxembourg, Romania
1993: v Faeroes(2), Belgium(2), Czechoslovakia
1994: v Czechoslovakia, Cyprus, Romania
1995: v Albania, Bulgaria
1996: v Germany, Albania, San Marinov San Marino, Turkey, Belgium
1997: v Turkey, Belgium
1998: v Italy(2), Denmark.

Although he was born in Cardiff, Ryan Giggs was brought up in Manchester where his father played Rugby League after a successful career in Rugby Union. Then known as Ryan Wilson, he was actually at Manchester City's School of Excellence and captained England Schoolboys against Scotland at Old Trafford before United snapped him up as a trainee in the summer of 1990.

It was around this time that his mother changed her name to Giggs and though Ryan's talent was obvious, United were careful to develop him slowly. They were reluctant to throw him into the first team week after week and it wasn't until 1992 that he became a permanent member of the United side.

He made his league debut for United as a substitute against Everton at Old Trafford in March 1991 and played just once more that season in the local derby against Manchester City on 4 May 1991, when he scored the only goal of the game.

His appearance as a substitute for Wales in their European Championship qualifying game against Germany in Nuremberg on 16 October 1991 made him the youngest-ever player to be capped by his country - at just 17 years and 321 days old. It's a feat which puts him alongside two other United players - Duncan Edwards, who was the youngest Englishman to be capped and Norman Whiteside who achieved a similar distinction for Northern Ireland.

Giggs' first full international debut for Wales came in 1993 in the World Cup qualifier against Belgium when he slammed a free-kick from outside the penalty area into the roof of the net for Wales' opening goal.

He set another record when he became the first player to win the PFA's Young Player of the Year Award in successive seasons, a feat he achieved in 1991-92 and 1992-93.

Giggs is blessed with the pace to outstrip most full-backs and the two-footed ability to go inside or outside his marker whenever he chooses. He also has the confidence and the power to go on and finish his own good work when the opportunity arises and has scored a number of spectacular goals.

In 1996 at the age of 22, he became the youngest player to appear in two double-winning sides - the first he won with United in 1994, aged 20.

One of his greatest games for United came in the 1996-97 season against

Ryan Giggs

Porto at Old Trafford, a performance that was compared with George Best's legendary night against Benfica some thirty-one years earlier.

In 1998-99, he scored the all-important equaliser against Juventus in the European Cup semi-final at Old Trafford before netting after a wondrous 60-yard run against Arsenal in the FA Cup semi-final replay. It prompted United manager Sir Alex Ferguson to say 'It was the goal of a genius', whilst Ryan described it as probably the best he has scored for the club !

During his nine seasons at Old Trafford, Giggs has suffered his fair share of injuries - broken nose, hamstring, broken left foot - but happily they seem to be a thing of the past for a player who seems to have the near-perfect temperament to cope with anything and everything that comes his way.

There is no finer sight in football than to see Ryan Giggs tearing down the left flank in search of goals. Now at the peak of his form, he was an inspirational figure during United's treble-winning season.

One of the game's most talked about players, he has won five Premier League Championship medals, three FA Cup winners' medals, a League Cup winners' medal and a European Cup winners' medal in his Old Trafford career.

BARRIE HOLE

Birthplace   Swansea
Born   16 September 1942

Football League Career

	Appearances	Goals
Cardiff City	211	16
Blackburn Rovers	79	13
Aston Villa	47	6
Swansea City	78	3

30 caps:
1963: (Cardiff.C) v N.Ireland
1964: v N.Ireland

1965: v Scotland, Denmark, England, Greece(2) N.Ireland, Italy, USSR
1966: v England, USSR, Scotland, Denmark, N.Ireland, Brazil(2) Chile
1967: (Blackburn.R) v Scotland, England, N.Ireland
1968: v England, Scotland, N.Ireland, W.Germany
1969: (Aston Villa) v Italy, W.Germany, E.Germany
1970: v Italy
1971: (Swansea.C) v Romania

The son of pre-war Welsh international winger Billy Hole, a Swansea Town player, his two older brothers, Colin and Alan both followed in their father's footsteps and played for their home-town club.

Barrie Hole did not follow the family tradition, preferring to join neighbours and rivals Cardiff City. He made his league debut for the Bluebirds as a 17-year-old in a 4-3 win at Leyton Orient on 27 February 1960, a season in which the Ninian Park club won promotion to the First Division. After getting another first team chance the following season, he established himself as a creative wing-half and inside-forward although he occasionally turned out at centre-forward in an injury crisis. Hole rarely missed a game, being ever-present in 1964-65. Whilst at Ninian Park, Hole won five Welsh Under-23 caps and won the first of 30 full caps when he played against Northern Ireland in 1963.

During the summer of 1966, Hole was allowed to leave Cardiff and joined Blackburn Rovers for a fee of £40,000. He was the Lancashire club's first specialist midfielder in the days when tactics were changing in the wake of England's World Cup triumph. Tall and slight in build, Hole was an extraordinarily gifted ball player. His intelligent positioning and constructive use of the ball made him one of the most exciting midfield players of his era. Not affected by pre-match nerves, he had the ability to ghost into the opposing penalty area completely free from markers, enabling him to score a number of important goals.

In September 1968, Hole was on the move again, this time to Aston Villa for £60,000. Though he admitted to a fear of flying, Hole rather surprisingly put his international career in jeopardy when he flew to play in America with the Villa Park club rather than represent Wales in the 1970 Home International Championships. Hole's time at Villa Park was not a happy one and midway through the 1969-70 season, he quit the club following a stormy time under Tommy Docherty's management. In fact, Hole turned his back on the game and went into his father's business.

During the summer of 1970, Roy Bentley the Swansea manager persuaded him to make a comeback, willingly paying Villa £20,000 to bring Hole to the Vetch Field.

An important member of the Swans' midfield for a couple of seasons, he left the game in May 1972 and like his father before him, became a newsagent in Swansea.

MEL HOPKINS

Birthplace   Rhondda
Born   7 November 1934

Football League Career

	Appearances	Goals
Tottenham Hotspur	219	0
Brighton and Hove Albion	57(1)	2
Bradford Park Avenue	29(1)	0

34 caps:
1956: (Tottenham.H) v N.Ireland
1957: v Scotland, England, N.Ireland, Czechoslovakia(2) E.Germany
　　　　1958: v E.Germany, England, Scotland, Israel(2) N.Ireland,
　　　Hungary(2) Mexico, Sweden, Brazil
1959: v Scotland, England, N.Ireland
1960: v England, Scotland
1961: v N.Ireland, Spain(2) Hungary
1962: v N.Ireland, Brazil(2) Mexico
1963: v Scotland, N.Ireland, Hungary

Mel Hopkins grew up in a Rhondda rugby stronghold where as a boy he had to form his own team to get a game of soccer. He was spotted by both Spurs and Manchester United playing for the Ystrad Boys Club in Glamorgan and was offered the chance to join the groundstaff of either club. He chose the White Hart Lane club and after developing rapidly, made his league debut against Derby County in October 1952, six months after signing professional forms. It was another two years before he was able to replace the ageing Arthur Willis and Charlie Withers as first-choice left-back but by the mid 1950s, Hopkins was recognised as one of the best full-backs in the country. Fast, tenacious and strong in the tackle, Hopkins liked nothing better than joining the attack but was always able to recover quickly when circumstances required it.

He made his international debut against Northern Ireland at Ninian Park in April 1956, being first-choice for Wales for several years and making 23 successive appearances. He played for his country throughout the World Cup Finals of 1958, helping them reach the quarter-finals where he gave a near faultless display against the Brazilian winger Garrincha.

It was whilst playing for Wales against Scotland at Hampden Park in November 1959 that Mel Hopkins' nose was horrifically smashed in a collision with the home side's Ian St John. The injury not only cost Hopkins his place in the Welsh side but also his position in Bill Nicholson's Spurs' side who were on the threshold of greatness. His place in the Tottenham side was taken by Ron Henry who took his chance so well that he wore the number three shirt throughout the club's 1960-61 League and Cup double season. Though he remained at White Hart Lane for a further five seasons, Hopkins was never able to get back into the Spurs team on a regular basis. His only goal for the club in 240 first team appearances came in his only European encounter as Spurs beat Slovan Bratislava 6-0 in March 1963. Though he was primarily a reserve during his last few seasons with the White Hart Lane club, he was still first-choice for Wales and in total won 34 caps, plus one at Under-23 level.

In October 1964 he followed Spurs striker Bobby Smith to Brighton and Hove Albion and played an important role in helping the Seagulls win that season's Fourth Division Championship. On leaving the Goldstone Ground, Hopkins played for Ballymena, Canterbury City and later Bradford Park Avenue where he took his total of Football League appearances for his three clubs to 307.

He eventually became a sports instructor for the Brighton Education Authority and then Sports Officer of the Horsham Sports Centre.

MARK HUGHES

Birthplace	Wrexham
Born	1 November 1963

Football League Career

	Appearances	Goals
Manchester United	336(9)	119
Chelsea	88(7)	25
Southampton	32	1

72 caps: 16 goals
1984   (Manchester.U) v England, N.Ireland
1986 v Iceland(2), Spain(2), Norway(2), Scotland
1987   (Barcelona) v Hungary, Uruguay
1988 v USSR, Czechoslovakia v Denmark(2) Czechoslovakia, Sweden, Malta, Italy
1989   (Manchester.U) v Holland, Finland, Israel, Sweden, W.Germany
        1990 v Finland, W.Germany, Costa Rica
1991 v Denmark, Belgium(2) Luxembourg, Iceland, Poland, West Germany
1992 v Brazil, Germany, Luxembourg, Republic of Ireland, Romania, Holland, Argentina, Japan 1992
1993 v Faeroe Islands(2) Cyprus, Belgium(2) Republic of Ireland, Czechoslovakia
1994 v Czechoslovakia, Cyprus, Norway
1995 v Georgia (2), Germany, Bulgaria
1996   (Chelsea) v Moldova, Italy, San Marino
1997 v San Marino, Holland, Turkey, Republic of Ireland, Belgium
1998 v Turkey (Southampton) v Italy (2), Denmark (2), Belarus, Sweden

Mark Hughes first caught Manchester United's eye while playing for Wrexham Schoolboys and on leaving school joined the Old Trafford groundstaff as an apprentice midfield player. But it was his conversion to a forward, partnering Norman Whiteside in United's successful youth team which stamped him as a star of the future.

Unlike Whiteside, he had to wait to make his impact but scored on his league debut in a 2-0 win over Leicester City in March 1984. He made a highly encouraging start, scoring four goals in his seven full appearances that season. He also played in United's European Cup Winners' Cup tie against Barcelona at the Nou Camp Stadium before crowning a remarkable first season by scoring on his Welsh debut against England at the Racecourse Ground.

The following season he was United's number one striker, scoring 25 goals in all competitions, the best individual scoring performance at Old Trafford for thirteen years. He hit two hat-tricks during this campaign, against Aston Villa in the League and Barnsley in the League Cup but it wasn't just the number of goals he scored that made it a special season, it was the style of them. The glorious leaping volley which flew past Luis Arconada in a World Cup qualifying match against Spain will linger long in the memory. He not only scored superb goals that season, but vital ones as well - that goal against Spain and the winner in the FA Cup semi-final against Liverpool when he broke clear to beat Bruce Grobbelaar with a perfectly placed low shot. He ended the campaign with an FA Cup winners' medal as United beat Everton and not surprisingly was voted the PFA Young Player of the Year.

At the start of the 1985-86 season, United went fifteen games before suffering their first defeat - Hughes scored 10 goals in that run as the Reds raced to the top of the table and into a commanding lead. It is little wonder that Hughes soon had every scout in Europe coming to Old Trafford to see his talents. However, after results fell away, it was announced that 'Sparky' was to be sold to Barcelona for £2.3 million - many supporters were angry and saw the sale as a betrayal. Hughes though managed to keep a foothold in the Old Trafford camp, stating that when he did come back to England, he would only join one club, that being Manchester United.

In fact, Hughes found Spanish football difficult and in his second season, he was sent out on loan to Bayern Munich in Germany, where he was much happier. Whilst with the German club, Hughes was the subject of a somewhat frantic attempt by both Wales and Bayern Munich to ensure that he played for both teams on the same day. So on 11 November 1987, he played for Wales against Czechoslovakia in Prague in a European Championship match before being rushed from the changing room to a waiting car which took him to a waiting plane. He reached Bayern's Olympic Stadium with the match already underway but went on in the second-half to help his team to victory !

United manager Alex Ferguson wanted to sign Hughes just before Barcelona loaned him to Bayern Munich but in June 1988 he clinched the deal on a player that many felt should never have been allowed to leave Old Trafford in the first place.

After an understandably low-key start on his return to the United side, he began to re-adjust to English football. He finished his first season back at Old Trafford as United's leading scorer with 14 goals including eight in a nine-match spell. He was duly honoured by his peers when he was elected Player of the Year by the Professional Footballers' Association.

He added a second FA Cup winners' medal to his collection in 1990 as United beat Crystal Palace, Hughes hitting a couple of goals in the first drawn game. In 1991 Hughes was part of the Manchester United team which became the first English side to win a European trophy after the Heysel ban. He scored the crucial goal too as the Reds beat his old club Barcelona 2-1 to lift the European Cup Winners' Cup in Rotterdam. Also that year, he became the only British player to have twice been voted the PFA Player of the Year.

A great favourite with the United fans, his £1.5 million move to Chelsea in the summer of 1995 came as a great shock, particularly as he was thought to have signed a two-year contract at Old Trafford. Hughes received a rapturous ovation when he returned there with Chelsea in a campaign which saw him score his first hat-trick for the Stamford Bridge club in a 4-1 thrashing of Leeds United.

The following season he formed an almost telepathic understanding with Gianfranco Zola but was remarkably left on the bench by Ruud Gullit

Mark Hughes

for the fourth round FA Cup match against Liverpool. At half-time with the Blues 2-0 down, Gullit brought on Hughes and within five minutes he had reduced the deficit. Leading the line magnificently, he led his side to a remarkable 4-2 win. In a campaign in which he was the club's leading scorer, he created a twentieth century record with his fourth FA Cup winners' medal following Chelsea's 2-0 win over Middlesbrough.

He began the 1997-98 season in great form, scoring against Manchester United in the Charity Shield at Wembley. He also scored against them in the League - his first goal at Old Trafford since joining Chelsea. Awarded the MBE in the 1998 New Year's Honours List he helped the Blues win the European Cup Winners' Cup before being signed by Southampton for £500,000 in July of that year.

His decision to move to The Dell came as the competition for striking places at Chelsea had increased and he felt he could not command a regular Premiership place.

In the event he has probably made more appearances for his new club in midfield than he has as a striker, his strength on the ball helping the Saints avoid relegation. Still a regular in the Welsh side he was appointed his country's national team manager in 1999.

LEIGHTON JAMES

Birthplace	Llwchwr, nr Swansea
Born	16 February 1953

Football League Career

	Appearances	Goals
Burnley	331(5)	66
Derby County	67(1)	15
Queen's Park Rangers	27(1)	4
Swansea City	88(10)	27
Sunderland	50(2)	4
Bury	46	5
Newport County	21(7)	2

54 caps: 10 goals.
1972 (Burnley) v Czechoslovakia, Romania, Scotland
1973 v England(3), Poland, Scotland, N.Ireland
1974 v Poland, England, Scotland, N.Ireland
1975 v Austria, Hungary(2), Luxembourg(2), Scotland, England, N.Ireland
1976 v Austria (Derby.C) v Yugoslavia(2), Scotland, England, N.Ireland
1977 v W.Germany, Scotland(2), Czechoslovakia, England, N.Ireland
1978 v Kuwait(2) (Queen's Park Rangers) v W.Germany
1979 (Burnley) v Turkey
1980 (Swansea.C) v England, Scotland, N.Ireland, Iceland
1981 v Turkey(2) Republic of Ireland, Scotland, England
1982 v Iceland, Czechoslovakia, USSR, England, Scotland, N.Ireland, France
1983 (Sunderland) v England

One of the game's most naturally gifted players, Leighton James was a winger of great speed and skill and always had an eye for goal.

The son of a steelworker, Leighton James represented Swansea Boys and was then chosen for the Welsh Schoolboy international team but he could quite easily have emerged as a Welsh Rugby Union international, excelling as he did in both codes during his schooldays. As it was he opted for Association Football and in October 1968 he signed apprentice forms for Burnley. After turning professional on his 17th birthday, he made his League debut for the Clarets in a 2-1 win over Nottingham Forest in November 1970 but at the end of that campaign in which he made four further first team appearances, the Turf Moor club were relegated to the Second Division. Still eligible for the club's youth team, he helped the young Clarets to reach the semi-final of the FA Youth Cup.

In 1971-72, James established himself as a regular in the Burnley side, his performances in the number 11 shirt alerting the national selectors. James won the first of his 54 caps as a substitute in the European Championship match against Czechoslovakia in Prague in October 1971 and at 18 years 238 days old, was one of the youngest players to appear for

Wales in a full international.

He was ever-present in 1972-73, a season in which the magical Welshman became a household name. The campaign saw Burnley crowned as Second Division Champions and though BBC's 'Match of the Day' featured a number of the Clarets' brilliant performances, it was Leighton James' exhibition of wing play that caught the eye. After two good seasons in the top flight and an appearance in the 1974-75 FA Cup semi-final against Newcastle United, James became unsettled and in November 1975 he joined Derby County for £310,000.

He spent two seasons at the Baseball Ground but despite being the club's top scorer in 1976-77 with 15 goals, he didn't seem to figure in new manager Tommy Docherty's plans and in October 1977 he went to Queen's Park Rangers in an exchange deal which saw Don Masson go to Derby. However, within less than a year, James was back at his beloved Turf Moor as Burnley manager Harry Potts paid out £165,000 for his services, a record fee that stood until 1994.

In his second spell with the Clarets, James was instrumental in them winning the Anglo-Scottish Cup in 1978 but two years later, following the club's relegation to the Third Division, James moved on again, this time to ambitious Swansea City for a fee of £130,000.

With his hunched shoulders and that unmistakable loping run with total control over the ball, James was a big favourite with the Swansea fans. In his first season at Vetch Field, he was the club's leading scorer as the Swans finished third in Division Two and so gain promotion to the top flight for the first time in the club's history. He also played a major role in City's victory in the Welsh Cup with its passport to European football. Although the Swans were knocked out in the first round of the Cup Winners' Cup, their season in Division One was a great success with James playing a leading role.

In January 1983, James moved to Sunderland on a free transfer, helping to spark something of a revival at Roker Park. Halting the Wearsiders' slide towards relegation, the club finished the season in a respectable mid-table position.

In the summer of 1984, James returned to Lancashire to team up with Bury who were managed by another former Claret in Martin Dobson.

Leighton James

James was also an integral member of the Swansea side that took the old First Division by storm in 1981-82 when the Welsh club's displays not only captured the imagination of the locals but the whole country as Arsenal, Liverpool and Manchester United were amongst the sides that came a cropper at Vetch Field. James finished the season as the club's leading goalscorer with 14 in the League and the Swans finished sixth in the table.

James had scored 99 goals in 394 league games for Swansea when in July 1983 after the club had lost their place in the top flight, he joined Stoke City for £160,000. Unfortunately he never quite showed the same form for the Potters that made him a regular and passionate Welsh international and manager Bill Asprey offloaded James to Queen's Park Rangers in October 1984 for £100,000.

At Loftus Road he was used successfully as a full-back before moving to Leicester City in June 1987. Bryan Hamilton, the Foxes manager saw in Robbie James the sort of experienced campaigner who could help settle a predominantly young Second Division defence, but sadly many of his efforts were negated by a lack of pace.

After Wales had been eliminated from the European Championships, James seemed to lose some of his enthusiasm for the game and in January 1988 he was released and returned to the Vetch Field for a second spell.

Immediately assuming the captaincy, he led the Swans to promotion from the Fourth Division via the 1988 play-offs and scored in their Welsh Cup win of 1989. James was transferred to Bradford City in August 1990 as part of a deal involving Alan Davies in settlement of the Welsh club's outstanding court action against manager Terry Yorath. After leaving Valley Parade, James celebrated a further Championship success with Cardiff City's Division Three side of 1993, where he also picked up his fifth Welsh Cup-winners' medal.

His move to non-League Merthyr Tydfil as the club's player-manager prompted the first instance of the FA of Wales convening a transfer tribunal to set the £10,000 fee and closed his Football League career on 782 appearances, a total only bettered by Peter Shilton, Terry Paine and Tommy Hutchison. After playing for Barry Town, Robbie James joined Llanelli for whom he was playing in a Welsh League game when he tragically collapsed and died, aged just 40.

BRYN JONES

Birthplace   Merthyr Tydfil
Born   14 February 1912
Died   18 October 1985

Football League Career

	Appearances	Goals
Wolverhampton Wanderers	163	52
Arsenal	71	7
Norwich City	23	1

17 caps: 6 goals.
1935   (Wolverhampton.W) v N.Ireland
1936 v England, Scotland, N.Ireland
1937 v England, Scotland, N.Ireland
1938 v England, Scotland, N.Ireland
1939   (Arsenal) v England, Scotland, N.Ireland
1947 v Scotland, N.Ireland
1948 v England
1949 v Scotland

In August 1938, Bryn Jones became the costliest footballer in Great Britain when he was transferred from Wolverhampton Wanderers to Arsenal for a fee of £14,000.

But surprisingly for such a 'valuable' player, Bryn Jones' career prior to him joining the Molineux club in November 1933 had been rather circuitous.

After leaving Queen's Road School in Merthyr Tydfil, he had a brief spell down the pit before turning out for both Merthyr Amateurs and Plymouth Albion in the local South Wales District League. His performances led to him having a trial for Southend United but after being unsuccessful, he teamed up with Irish club Glenavon. In the summer of 1933 he returned to Wales to play for Aberaman but after just a handful of games, Wolves had paid £1,500 for his services. From that moment on, Bryn Jones became a star.

He made his debut for Wolves in a 2-1 win over Everton at Goodison Park and ended his first campaign with 10 goals in 27 games. In his second season with the club, he won the first of 17 Welsh caps when he played against Northern Ireland. Jones, who was a wonderful ball player and always aware of what was happening elsewhere on the pitch, stayed at Molineux for five seasons, scoring 57 goals in 177 games including a hatrick in a 4-2 home win over Preston North End on 20 April 1936. His best season in terms of goals scored was 1937-38 when he netted 15 in 36 league games but at the end of that campaign, he left to join Arsenal.

He had become a firm favourite with the Wolves' fans and they were bitterly disappointed when he was allowed to leave for Highbury.

Although the Gunners had won the League Championship in 1937-38, £the club management were not happy, for they could not find a ready replacement for Alex James, until now ! Up to that point, no player had been under such media attention and Jones was rather unkindly dubbed 'the new James'. With war just around the corner, the little Welshman had little time to show his talents. However, he scored Arsenal's opening goal on his debut in a 2-0 win over Portsmouth and followed this by scoring twice in the next three league games. Arsenal ended the season in fifth place and though some Gunners' fans blamed Jones for the club's lack of success in that campaign, it was most unfair.

Jones was a quiet, modest figure who could not cope with the intense pressure of the media spotlight even though on the field of play, his good positional awareness and splendid ball control were there for everyone to see.

During the Second World War, he was posted to Italy and North America whilst serving with the Royal Artillery.

On his return to Highbury in 1946, Jones was 34, but he began to reveal his true form and in 1947-48, helped the Gunners to win the League Championship. Though not a prolific scorer, he netted one of Arsenal's goals in the 4-3 Charity Shield victory over Manchester United. His Arsenal career finished whilst on the summer tour of Brazil in 1949 when unfortunately in a game against Vasco de Gama, spectators kept running on the pitch and accidentally or not, he was hit over the head by a Brazilian policeman !

On leaving Highbury, he became player-coach of Norwich City but after making 23 league appearances for the Canaries, he was recommended on doctor's advice to retire from the game.

Though he was only 5ft 6ins tall and topped the scales at under 11 stone, Bryn Jones used to fight it out on the park with the toughest of characters in the game. Also, when he was at Molineux, he would stand up to Major Frank Buckley - a thing very few Wolves players would do !

In September 1951, he took over a newsagent-tobacconist shop near Highbury and here he stayed for some considerable time, before his death at the age of 73 in 1985.

CLIFF JONES

Birthplace   Swansea
Born   7 February 1935

Football League Career

	Appearances	Goals
Swansea City	168	47
Tottenham Hotspur	314(4)	135
Fulham	23(2)	2

59 caps: 16 goals.
1954   (Swansea) v Austria
1956 v England, Scotland, Austria, N.Ireland
1957 v Scotland, England, N.Ireland, E.Germany, Czechoslovakia(2)
1958 v E.Germany, England, Scotland, Israel(2), (Tottenham.H) v
       N.Ireland, Hungary(2), Mexico, Sweden, Brazil
1959 v N.Ireland
1960 v England, Scotland, N.Ireland
1961 v Republic of Ireland, Scotland, England, N.Ireland, Spain,
       Hungary
1962 v England, Scotland, N.Ireland, Brazil(2), Mexico
1963 v Scotland, Hungary, N.Ireland
1964 v England, Scotland, N.Ireland

1965 v Scotland, Denmark, England, Greece(2), N.Ireland, Italy, USSR
1967 v Scotland, England
1968 v England, Scotland, W.Germany
1969   (Fulham) v Italy
1970 v Rest of UK

One of Wales' greatest-ever players, Cliff Jones was the fourth member of his family to make his name in professional football, following his father Ivor, who played for Swansea Town, West Bromwich Albion and Wales, his uncle Bryn, who played for Wolverhampton Wanderers, Arsenal, Norwich City and Wales and his brother Bryn, who played for Swansea Town, Newport County, Bournemouth, Northampton Town and Watford.

In his youth, he played for both Swansea and Wales School's sides and in 1949-50 captained the Swansea Schoolboys team that won the English Schools Shield for the second time since the war.

Though he was taken onto the staff at the Vetch Field, he was wise enough to learn a trade outside football, that of a sheet metal worker at the Swansea Docks.

He made his first team debut for the Swans as a 17-year-old in October 1952 at inside-forward but was later persuaded by Swansea trainer Joe Sykes to switch to the wing. Jones never looked back, his form led to him winning the first of 59 caps for Wales when he played against Austria in May 1954. He had a disappointing debut and had to wait another eighteen months before being given another chance, this time against England at Ninian Park. It was a completely different story with Wales winning 2-1 and Cliff Jones scoring a memorable goal.

His performances for both club and country led to a number of top clubs making inquiries about him but just when it seemed as if he would leave the Vetch, he had to do two years National Service which had been deferred because of his apprenticeship in the Royal Horse Artillery (King's Troop).

On returning to Swansea, he was eventually signed by Tottenham Hotspur, who after a long series of negotiations, paid £35,000 to take him to White Hart Lane. After just three months with Spurs he was off to

Cliff Jones

Rotherham United in January 1973. The Llandudno-born full-back went on to play in 118 first team games before Liverpool manager Bob Paisley paid £110,000 for him in the summer of 1975.

Signed to replace the out of form Alec Lindsay, his early displays for the Anfield club indicated too many rough edges for the top flight. Phil Neal switched to left-back and Tommy Smith came in on the right, Jones was out of the side. That disappointment however was merely a prelude to his finest season with the club, that of 1976-77. Having won a regular place in the Liverpool side, he went on to help them win that season's European Cup and League Championship, whilst they also just missed out on the FA Cup, losing 2-1 to Manchester United. During the club's run to the European Cup Final, the Kopites took the tattooed Jones to their hearts. After victories over the French, Swiss and West German champions, the Liverpool fans coined the catchphrase 'Who ate the Frogs' legs, made the Swiss roll and topped the lot by munching Gladbach?' to immortalise Jones' displays in the Liverpool defence.

His performances led to him winning the first of 72 caps for Wales when he played against Austria at the Racecourse Ground, a match the Welsh won 1-0. His total of international appearances was a Welsh record until broken by Peter Nicholas in 1991.

Jones lost his place in the Liverpool side when manager Bob Paisley shuffled the Reds' defence to accommodate the increasingly impressive Alan Hansen. So it came as no surprise when he returned to Wrexham in September 1978 for a club record fee of £210,000.

Jones' first season in his second spell at the Racecourse Ground was the club's first in the Second Division. He stayed for four years but after the club were relegated in 1981-82, he discovered that his international place was in jeopardy and so he left the Racecourse Ground to link up with his former manager John Neal at Chelsea.

During his three years at Stamford Bridge, Jones won a Second Division Championship medal before leaving to play for Huddersfield Town. Whilst with the Terriers, Jones broke Ivor Allchurch's long standing record of Welsh international appearances when he played his 69th game for Wales against the Republic of Ireland in March 1986. He had previously announced his retirement from the international scene but with Mike

Joey Jones

England's squad decimated through injuries, he offered to help out.

In August 1987, Jones again became a Wrexham player for the ridiculously low fee of £7,000 and in 1988-89 helped the club reach the Fourth Division promotion play-off finals where they lost to Leyton Orient.

In December 1989, Wrexham manager Brian Flynn made Jones the club's player-coach and after playing the last of his 482 first team games for the Robins at home to Chesterfield in November 1991, he has since concentrated on coaching.

Jones, who had a special rapport with the fans at most of his clubs, was voted Player of the Year at Chelsea, Huddersfield and Wrexham.

TOMMY G. JONES

Birthplace	Connahs Quay
Born	12 October 1917

Football League Career

	Appearances	Goals
Wrexham	6	0
Everton	165	4

17 caps:
1938 (Everton) v N.Ireland
1939 v England, Scotland, N.Ireland
1947 v England, Scotland
1948 v England, Scotland, N.Ireland
1949 v England, N.Ireland, Portugal, Belgium, Sweden
1950 v England, Scotland, Belgium

A constructive player who always attempted to use the ball, Tommy Jones began his Football League career with Wrexham whom he joined from non-League Llanerch Celtic but after just seven first team appearances for the Robins, he left the Racecourse Ground in March 1936 and joined Everton for £3,000.

He made his debut for the Blues six months later in a 1-0 defeat at Leeds United but it was his only game of the season. Jones established himself in the Everton side the following season, 1937-38, at the end of which he won the first of 17 Welsh caps when he played against Northern Ireland at Belfast. He won a League Championship medal in 1938-39 but when the war came, he was at his peak.

Jones was a defender with the style of an inside-forward. At a time when Arsenal with their 'stopper' boasted a prototype in defensive standards, Jones refused to be screwed into the six-yard line.

Standing 6ft 1 ins and weighing just under 14 stone, Jones always played his way out of trouble. His fame was international but without doubt the biggest compliment he was ever paid came from Everton goalscoring legend Dixie Dean, who named Tommy Jones as the greatest footballer he had ever seen. Jones had everything, no coach could ever coach him or teach him anything. He could get himself out of trouble just by running towards the ball and then letting it run between his legs, knowing that a team-mate would be in a position to take it. He also had the great capacity to stroke the ball around. Possessing the best right foot in the business, his positioning and balance was so complete that he always seemed to receive the ball on his favoured right foot.

During the war years, he appeared in 142 games for the club and when League football resumed in 1946-47, he was again Everton's first-choice pivot, scoring his first goal in the 3-2 defeat by Sheffield United. He was appointed club captain in August 1949, succeeding Peter Farrell but a year earlier he could well have left Goodison Park.

Italian giants AS Roma made desperate and prolonged attempts to sign the Everton and Wales centre-half and though the Merseyside club initially accepted a considerable fee, the deal fell through after a row over the currency transaction.

Towards the end of his career, Jones upset the Everton board by publicly expressing his concern at the way the club was being run. He eventually moved to Pwllheli where he was appointed player-manager.

FRED KEENOR

Birthplace   Cardiff
Born   21 July 1894
Died   19 October 1972

Football League Career
	Appearances	Goals
Cardiff City	369	10
Crewe Alexandra	116	5

32 caps: 2 goals.
1920   (Cardiff.C) v Ireland, England
1921 v Scotland, England, Ireland
1922 v Ireland
1923 v England, Scotland, Ireland
1924 v Scotland, England, Ireland
1925 v Scotland, England, N.Ireland
1926 v Scotland
1927 v Scotland, England, N.Ireland
1928 v Scotland, England, N.Ireland
1929 v Scotland, England, N.Ireland
1930 v Scotland, England, N.Ireland
1931 v Scotland, England, N.Ireland
1933   (Crewe.A) v Scotland

After having been capped at outside-right in 1907 in the first schoolboy international between Wales and England, Fred Keenor joined his home-town team Cardiff City as an amateur inside-forward four years later in the club's pre-First World War Southern League days. He turned professional in the summer of 1912 and made his first team debut for the Bluebirds in a 1-1 home draw against Exeter City in December 1913. At the outbreak of the First World War, Keenor joined the 'Footballers Battalion' (17th Middlesex) and was twice wounded in action. At the end of the hostilities, he returned to Ninian Park and

Fred Keenor

made his first appearance for Wales in the Victory internationals.

When the Bluebirds entered the Football League, Fred Keenor scored in the club's first league game, a 5-2 win at Stockport County. Succeeding Charlie Brittan as captain, he led both his club and country to success. He led Wales to the Home International Championship in 1924 and a year later took Cardiff to an unsuccessful FA Cup Final, the Bluebirds losing 1-0 to Sheffield United. The Ninian Park club were very disappointing and in a post-match statement, Fred Keenor apologised for their performance and absolved half-back Harry Wake, who was caught in possession, of causing the club's downfall. He also vowed that City would return to Wembley and win the trophy !

He was as good as his word, for in 1927, the Bluebirds did return to the Twin Towers where they beat Arsenal 1-0. Keenor at right-half never put a foot wrong throughout the game, as Charlie Buchan the Arsenal skipper later recalled - 'I can still remember Fred's great display on that occasion, he marshalled his men magnificently....his store of energy seemed inexhaustible in defending his goal and supplying his forwards with crisp passes.'

Fred Keenor was one of the hardest tacklers in the game and this coupled with his will to win, made him a tough opponent. There were some that said Fred Keenor was dirty, but he was just hard. And he was certainly fit considering he was virtually a chain smoker. He would often lap Ninian Park in a pair of old heavy army boots whilst his team-mates were doing ball practice.

Keenor, who made 32 appearances for his country, was an inspirational leader. In October 1930 he captained the 'Unknowns' when the bookmakers were prepared to offer odds on Scotland, after allowing Wales a five-goal start! Not surprisingly, Fred Keenor's fighting spirit and great enthusiasm guided the so-called no-hopers to a 1-1 draw.

He went on to appear in 436 League and Cup games for the Bluebirds, a club he had done much to establish before leaving to join Crewe Alexandra after nineteen years at Ninian Park.

In three years at Gresty Road, he made 116 first team appearances before going into non-League football, first with Oswestry and then as player-manager of Tunbridge Wells.

A serious illness ended the career of a man who had become a legend in Welsh football.

JACK KELSEY

Birthplace   Llansamlet, nr Swansea
Born   19 November 1929
Died   19 March 1992

Football League Career

	Appearances	Goals
Arsenal	327	0

41 caps:
1954   (Arsenal) v N.Ireland, Austria
1955 v Yugoslavia, Scotland, N.Ireland
1956 v England, Scotland, Austria, N.Ireland
1957 v Scotland, England, N.Ireland, Czechoslovakia(2), E.Germany 1957
1958 v England, Scotland, Israel(2) N.Ireland, Hungary(2) Mexico, Sweden, Brazil
1959 v Scotland, England
1960 v England, Scotland, N.Ireland
1961 v Scotland, England, N.Ireland, Spain(2) Hungary
1962 v England, Scotland, N.Ireland, Brazil(2)

Jack Kelsey holds Arsenal's goalkeeping appearances record and is the Gunners' most-capped Welshman.

A one-club man, Kelsey was unlucky to be at Highbury at a time when the club's fortunes were at a real low ebb. Although one of a long line of excellent custodians who have graced the Arsenal side over the years, he won just one club honour, a League Championship medal in his first full season and his distinguished career was ended prematurely by injury at the age of 32.

Born in Llansamlet near Swansea, Kelsey attended Cwm School. He was first inspired to become a goalkeeper after watching Billo Staddon who kept goal for local side Winch Wens in the late 1930s and then during the war, he was a regular spectator at the Vetch Field to watch Swansea's 'guest' 'keeper Fred Stansbridge.

30 caps: 6 goals.
1953   (Swansea) v N.Ireland, France, Yugoslavia
1957   (Tottenham.H) v Scotland, England, N.Ireland, Czechoslovakia(2), E.Germany
1958   v England, Scotland, Israel(2) N.Ireland, Hungary(2) Mexico, Brazil
1959   v Scotland, England, N.Ireland
1960   v England, Scotland, N.Ireland
1961   v Republic of Ireland, Scotland, England, Spain
1963   v Hungary, England

One of the heroes of Tottenham Hotspur's League and Cup 'double' winning side of 1960-61, Terry Medwin spent his childhood at Swansea Prison where his father, who was on Southampton's books in the 1920s, was a prison officer. Whilst playing for the Swansea and Wales Schools sides, his performances as a goalscoring winger attracted the attention of a number of top flight clubs but it was no real surprise when he joined the Vetch Field club next door to the prison !

After a few seasons of reserve team football, he made his league debut for the Swans in January 1952, scoring inside the first minute against Doncaster Rovers. He held his place for the rest of the season, alternating between the right-wing and centre-forward.

His form the following season led to him winning the first of 30 full caps for Wales when he played in a 3-2 win over Northern Ireland in Belfast in April 1953. Despite scoring regularly for the Swans over the next couple of seasons, he lost his place in the Welsh side. One of the game's most versatile players, having occupied all of the front line positions with the Vetch Field club, he joined Tottenham Hotspur on the last day of the 1955-56 season for £25,000. Medwin, who had scored 60 goals in 148 League games for Swansea, scored twice on his Spurs debut in a 6-0 home win over Leicester City.

His form in the First Division in 1956-57 led to him winning an international recall for the match against Scotland in October 1956. He scored in that game as Wales drew 2-2 and over the next five years became a regular in the side. Occasionally he was asked to replace John Charles at centre-forward, following the 'Gentle Giant's' move to Juventus but in the World Cup Finals of 1958, he formed a deadly partnership with Charles. During the vital play-off game against Hungary, Medwin scored one of the goals that took Wales into the quarter-finals, where despite Medwin again having an outstanding game, they lost 1-0 to Brazil.

Medwin, who was a Tottenham regular for four years, was most unfortunate to lose his first team place to Terry Dyson during the club's dramatic 1960-61 'double' winning season but with fifteen outings as deputy for either Dyson or Cliff Jones, he did qualify for a League Championship medal. The following season he appeared on a more regular basis and was a member of the Spurs side that retained the FA Cup, beating Burnley 3-1. Injuries sadly caused him to miss the club's European Cup Winners' Cup success over Athletico Madrid but he regained his fitness to tour South Africa with Spurs during the summer of 1963. It was on this trip that Medwin suffered a broken leg against a NSAFL Invitation XI.

After a long fight to regain full fitness, Terry Medwin eventually had to admit defeat and after scoring 96 goals in 247 games for the White Hart Lane club, he retired to take up the manager's post at Athenian League, Enfield. He later coached League sides, Cardiff City, Fulham and Norwich City as well as helping Dave Bowen with the Welsh team during the 1970s. Medwin's last appointment was back at the Vetch Field where he became assistant-manager to John Toshack. He helped the Swans reach the top flight but sadly in 1983, ill-health forced his premature retirement from the game.

BILLY MEREDITH

Birthplace   Black Park, nr Chirk
Born   30 July 1874
Died   19 April 1958

Football League Career

	Appearances	Goals
Northwich Victoria	6	0
Manchester City	367	146

Manchester United   303   35
48 caps: 11 goals.
1895   (Manchester.C) v Ireland, England
1896   v Ireland, England
1897   v Ireland, Scotland, England
1898   v Ireland, England
1899   v England
1900   v Ireland, England
1901   v England, Ireland
1902   v England, Scotland
1903   v England, Scotland, Ireland
1904   v England
1905   v Scotland, England
1907   (Manchester.U) v Ireland, Scotland, England
1908   v England, Ireland
1909   v Scotland, England, Ireland
1910   v Scotland, England, Ireland
1911   v Ireland, Scotland, England
1912   v Scotland, England, Ireland
1913   v Ireland, Scotland, England
1914   v Ireland, Scotland, England
1920   v Ireland, Scotland, England

The most famous of all Welsh footballers, Billy Meredith's figures are staggering. He played top-class football for no less than thirty years; from 1894 when at 19 he joined Manchester City from Chirk, his hometown just across the Shropshire-Wales border, to 1924 when he was accepted for every FA Cup tie in City's run up to the semi-final. He played in 367 League games for Manchester City and another 303, almost a career in itself for Manchester United between 1906 and 1921. He scored 181 League and 56 Cup goals.

The youngest of ten children, he won his first soccer medal at the age of ten when he took part in a dribbling competition. On leaving school at the age of 12, he went to work in the pits as a pony driver, continuing to work there for some time even after joining Manchester City.

Billy Meredith

Meredith played his early football for Wrexham in the Combination before breaking into the Football League with Northwich Victoria. His displays on the wing led to Manchester City making him an offer but he was reluctant to come to terms with the Hyde Road club and it took two days of discussion before City got their man.

He always spoke with amused irony at the nightmare week in which he won his first international cap in 1895. On the Saturday, after a desperate sea crossing, he played against Ireland in Belfast, then another night of sea-sickness on the way back; on the Monday, the game with England in London; on Tuesday, home to North Wales for a day's work down the pit (his Manchester City wages being insufficient to feed him and provide the allowance he paid his parents); on Wednesday, a League game for City; on Thursday and Friday, shifts down the pit; on the Saturday up the road to Wrexham to play for Wales against Scotland. For those internationals, Meredith was paid just **£1 a game (??)** !

It was money that led to his move to Manchester United in 1906, two years after he had scored the goal that gave City the FA Cup as Bolton Wanderers were beaten 1-0.

Eighteen City players, Meredith among them, were suspended for receiving 'illegal payments'. Immediately after the suspension, he moved to United and within three years, had won League and Cup medals with his new club.

Meredith was a prominent member of the Players' Union and a leading light in their struggle with the Football Association in 1909.

Meredith was selected for 71 consecutive international matches between 1895 and 1920 but because of the demands of his clubs, he was released for only 48 of them, plus the three Victory internationals in 1919. His last international appearance was in March 1920 when Wales met England at Highbury. The occasion was a special one even before the match started, for T.E.Thomas, Meredith's old headmaster at Chirk School was retiring. This remarkable man had introduced no fewer than 49 future Welsh internationals to football as pupils at his school and before the game a presentation was made to him by the five Chirk Old Boys in the Welsh team. Then, with 44-year-old Meredith tormenting the the home side, Wales beat England for the first time in their history.

The following year he returned to Manchester City, an incredible twenty-seven years after he had first worn their colours. His return match was against Aston Villa played at City's ground in Hyde Road. Meredith performed with much of his old audacity, delighting a crowd of over 35,000. Villa were beaten 2-1 and Meredith played a large part in the scoring of the first City goal.

Two years later as his fiftieth birthday approached, there was further proof of the veteran Welshman's remarkable stamina. Manchester City were at Ninian Park for an FA Cup tie but after ninety minutes, neither side had managed a goal in a match that had been played at a hectic pace. The game went into extra-time when Meredith completely outstripped his marker, less than half his age, crossed the ball with great accuracy for Browell to put the ball in the net and win the match for the Lancashire club. City went through to the semi-final but they were beaten 2-0 by Newcastle United.

By this time, Meredith had finally come to terms with his retirement. His final appearance came at the end of April 1925, by which time City were playing at Maine Road. That day, for his testimonial, a team of his own choosing played a combined Rangers and Celtic eleven. The game, a 2-2 draw was played with such panache that it was totally worthy of Meredith's achievements.

At an age when many coaches are contemplating retirement, Meredith joined their ranks. In 1931 he returned to Old Trafford in a coaching capacity, at a time when the club was going through a period of turmoil. He retained more affection for United than for the Maine Road club and throughout his later years, often visited the ground to watch the team in action. As late as 1950, funds were made available from Old Trafford to help him overcome a small financial problem.

Meredith, who was the first man to win both Welsh and FA Cup winners' medals, still holds the record as the oldest player to appear in an international match.

'Old Skinny' as he was popularly known, was said never to play without a toothpick in his mouth. His stamina remained in life as it had on the field and he was 81 when he died in 1958 just two months after the Munich air disaster.

GRENVILLE MORRIS

Birthplace
Born
Died

Football League Career

	Appearances	Goals
Nottingham Forest	423	199

21 caps: 9 goals.
1896   (Aberystwyth) v England, Ireland, Scotland
1897   (Swindon.T) v England
1898   v Scotland
1899   (Nottingham.F) v England, Scotland
1903   v England, Scotland
1905   v England, Scotland
1907   v England, Scotland
1908   v England
1910   v England, Scotland, Ireland
1911   v England, Scotland, Ireland
1912   v England

'The Prince of Inside-Forwards', Grenville Morris began his footballing career at St Oswald's College in Ellesmere, later moving on to Builth Town and then Aberystwyth. Morris was 18 when he won his first international cap for Wales, scoring one of the goals in a 6-1 win over Ireland at Wrexham.

With a promise of employment as a draughtsman at the local railway works, Morris signed for Southern League side, Swindon Town in the summer of 1897. The County Ground club considered Morris too light for the role of centre-forward and converted him into an inside-right. He had scored 16 goals in 29 games for the Robins when, within a year of his arrival at the County Ground, Nottingham Forest paid £200 for his services.

Morris, who made his Forest debut against Bury on 3 December 1898, became a regular goalscorer in his time with Forest. He topped the club's scoring charts in seven of his 15 seasons with the Reds.

He also scored five hat-tricks for Forest - West Bromwich Albion (Away 6-1 on 20 October 1900) Bury (Home 5-1 on 10 September 1904) Manchester City (Home 3-1 on 11 April 1908) Manchester United (Away 6-2 on 27 November 1909) and Sheffield Wednesday (Away 3-4 on 11 December 1909).

Morris, who had won two full caps for Wales whilst with Swindon, made a further sixteen appearances for his country during his days with Forest. Playing the last of his 460 League and Cup games for the City Ground club on 26 April 1913, scoring 217 goals, his tally of 199 League goals remains a record for Forest.

Grenville Morris was a very fit man, working in his own coal merchant's business. He was also a talented tennis player and was only forbidden from playing at Wimbledon because of his professional status.

PETER NICHOLAS

Birthplace	Newport	
Born	10 November 1959	

Football League Career

	Appearances	Goals
Crystal Palace	174	14
Arsenal	57(3)	1
Luton Town	102	1
Chelsea	79(1)	3
Watford	40	1

73 caps: 2 goals.
1979   (Crystal Palace) v Scotland, N.Ireland, Malta
1980 v   Republic of Ireland, W.Germany, Turkey, England, Scotland, N.Ireland, Iceland

1981 v Turkey(2), Czechoslovakia, Republic of Ireland, (Arsenal) v Scotland, England, USSR
1982 v Czechoslovakia, Iceland, USSR, Spain, England, Scotland, N.Ireland, France
1983 v Yugoslavia, Bulgaria, Scotland, N.Ireland
1984 v Norway(2) Bulgaria, Israel
1985   (Crystal Palace) v Spain (Luton.T) v Norway(2) Scotland, Spain
1986 v Scotland, Hungary, Saudi Arabia, Republic of Ireland, Uruguay, Canada(2)
1988 v USSR, Finland(2), Czechoslovakia, (Aberdeen) v Denmark(2) Czechoslovakia, Yugoslavia, Sweden
1989   (Chelsea) v Holland, Finland, Israel, Sweden, W.Germany
1990 v Finland, Holland, W.Germany, Republic of Ireland, Sweden, Costa Rica
1991 v Denmark, Belgium, Luxembourg, Republic of Ireland (Watford) v Belgium, Poland, Germany
1992 v Luxembourg 1992

Hard-tackling midfielder Peter Nicholas was a member of Crystal Palace's FA Youth Cup-winning sides. The Newport-born half-back, who gained Welsh Schools, Youth, Under-21 and full caps, signed professional forms in December 1976 and made his first team debut for Palace at Millwall on the opening day of the 1977-78 season in a 3-0 victory. Over the next four seasons, Nicholas was a virtual ever-present and helped Palace win promotion to the top flight as Second Division champions in 1978-79.

At one stage, Palace declared that Nicholas was positively the one player that would never be allowed to leave the South London club. But opinions and values change and after a while they were persuaded to part with their dominant midfield force. Nicholas was disillusioned by the managerial upheavals at Selhurst Park which saw Terry Venables leave and Dario Gradi take over. Those were turbulent times with Malcolm Allison and Ernie Walley in turn taking charge before Gradi's appointment.

A hard man in the mould of fearsome adversaries like Nobby Stiles and Peter Storey, Nicholas joined Arsenal in March 1981 for a fee of

Peter Nicholas

£400,000. Combining his natural toughness in the challenge with a deft skill and penchant for attacking, he quickly established himself as a favourite with the Highbury crowd.

When he arrived at Arsenal, the Gunners were wallowing ineffectively in mid-table and had won just three of their previous 14 League games. With Nicholas in the side, they proceeded to drop only two points in the last nine games of the season, moving up to third spot and claiming a place in Europe.

After making such a positive early impression, Nicholas was tipped for a long-term Highbury future but following two steady campaigns, he found himself on the sidelines as the Gunners' manager experimented with other players.

Nicholas moved back to Crystal Palace, originally on loan. He made more international appearances for Wales while playing for the Eagles but still registered with Arsenal, a fact which confuses the issue over whether he is Palace's most-capped player. Nicholas, who went on to assemble a record 73 Welsh international caps - since outstripped by Neville Southall and equalled by Ian Rush - eventually joined Palace on a permanent basis for a fee of £150,000 in October 1983. He had scored 16 goals in 199 games for the Selhurst Park club when following a row between Palace and the Welsh FA over injury payments, he left to join Luton Town in January 1985.

He later signed for Aberdeen for £350,000 and in 1987 became the first player from a Scottish club to be capped by Wales when he played against Denmark, since Freddie Warren in 1938.

In August 1988 following the illness of his child, Nicholas returned south to play for Chelsea. Appointed club captain, he played an important part in the Pensioners' promotion-winning season of 1988-89 when the Stamford Bridge club returned to the top flight as Second Division champions.

Nicholas later ended his League career with Watford before returning to Selhurst Park for a third spell as Crystal Palace's first team coach.

ROY PAUL

Birthplace   Ton Pentre
Born   18 April 1920

Football League Career

	Appearances	Goals
Swansea City	160	14
Manchester City	270	9

33 caps: 1 goal.
1949   (Swansea) v Scotland, England, N.Ireland, Portugal, Switzerland
1950 v   England, Scotland, Belgium, N.Ireland
1951   (Manchester.C) v Scotland, England, N.Ireland, Portugal, Switzerland
1952 v   England, Scotland, Rest of UK, N.Ireland
1953 v   Scotland, England, N.Ireland, France, Yugoslavia
1954 v   England, Scotland, N.Ireland
1955 v   Yugoslavia, Scotland, England
1956 v   England, Scotland, Austria, N.Ireland

Roy Paul was one of the greatest footballers to hail from the Rhondda during the 1940s, a forceful half-back who captained Manchester City to the FA Cup and made 33 appearances for Wales.

On leaving school, he began his working life in the mines, whilst still playing football at the weekends for a number of local sides. His performances attracted the attention of Swansea who, after acquiring his services as an amateur, quickly offered him professional terms. The Second World War intervened before the strong-tackling Paul could make his League debut but he was a regular in the club's wartime games, making some 84 appearances.

In 1940, Paul was called up for National Service and after being posted to Devon, 'guested' for Exeter City in wartime games. Following a particularly impressive display in a 3-1 win over Arsenal, he was ordered to report to the commanding officer. He arranged for Paul to go on a physical training

Roy Paul

course and he spent the rest of the war working as a PT instructor for the Marines in India.

After the hostilities, Paul returned to the Vetch Field and was a member of the Swansea side that was relegated to the Third Division at the end of the 1946-47 season. However two years later, he was instrumental in the club winning the Third Division (South) Championship, his performances leading to him winning his first international cap when he played against Scotland at Hampden Park. Whilst with Swansea his career almost took on an unlikely turn. British stars like Neil Franklin and Charlie Mitten were leading an exodus to Colombia where big money was on offer and this was soon extended to include Roy Paul. He was offered £3,000 to join Colombian club Millionairos but decided against joining them. Swansea were not impressed by Paul's trip to South America and transfer listed the Welsh international. A number of top flight clubs were interested in him but it was Manchester City who paid £25,000 for his services in the summer of 1950.

Paul made his debut for City in an attractive Maine Road clash against Preston North End on the opening day of the 1950-51 season. The Deepdale club, who ended up as Second Division champions that season, were beaten 4-2 and Paul who had been made captain by manager Les McDowall, had an outstanding game. Although City were unbeaten in the first ten games of the season, the manner in which that run came to an end was a taste of things to come. Leading Doncaster Rovers 3-0, courtesy of a George Smith hat-trick, City lost 4-3 to the Yorkshire side ! However, McDowall's investment was fully repaid when at the end of the season, City finished runners-up to North End to win promotion to the First Division.

Paul's first taste of top flight football was marked by inconsistency by City. After winning only two of their opening ten matches, McDowall signed Don Revie and Ivor Broadis and they, along with the strong tackling and accurate distribution of skipper Paul, were the main reasons City remained in Division One.

They reached the FA Cup Final at Wembley in 1955 only to lose 3-1 to Newcastle United. After the match the City skipper vowed that they would be back the following year and so it proved as the Maine Road club beat Birmingham 3-1. Thus, Roy Paul became one of the few Welshmen to captain an FA Cup winning side. In the close season he brought the FA Cup home to the Rhondda, fulfilling the promise he had made to take the trophy back to his native valleys. He woke one morning to find that he had left his car window open with the FA Cup lying on the back seat !

By the time of City's 1956 triumph, Paul's international career had reached its conclusion. His 33 caps included a single goals in a 5-1 win over Belgium but the highlight had come in his final season of international football when his eighth and last meeting with England brought a 2-1 win at Ninian Park, his only victory against the old enemy.

Paul's City career did not finish on such a high note. The 1956-57 season brought a familiar flirtation with relegation and it was only after a successful run towards the end of the campaign that City managed to finish as high as 18th.

Paul eventually left Maine Road on the advice of a doctor because his son suffered with his breathing and it was felt that the air would be cleaner away from the heavily industrialised city of Manchester.

His football career wound down with two seasons as player-manager of Worcester City but despite guiding them to an FA Cup fourth round tie with Sheffield United, he found the strain of travelling from South Wales too great.

On returning to the Rhondda, he became player-manager of Garw Athletic and worked as a lorry driver until he retired in the mid 1980s.

Though only an occasional visitor to Maine Road, he is far from forgotten and team-mate Ken Barnes is a regular caller, travelling to the Rhondda Valley in 1990 when Paul received an award for services to Welsh sport.

DAVID PHILLIPS

| Birthplace | Wegberg, Germany |
| Born | 29 July 1963 |

Football League Career

	Appearances	Goals
Plymouth Argyle	65(8)	15
Manchester City	81	13
Coventry City	93(7)	8
Norwich City	152	18
Nottingham Forest	116(10)	5
Huddersfield Town	44(8)	3
Lincoln City	9	0

62 caps: 2 goals.
1984   (Plymouth.A) v England, N.Ireland, Norway
1985   (Manchester.C) v Spain(2) Iceland, Scotland, Norway
1986 v Scotland, Hungary, Saudi Arabia, Republic of Ireland, Uruguay
1987   (Coventry.C) v Finland, Czechoslovakia
1988 v Denmark(2) Czechoslovakia, Yugoslavia, Sweden
1989 v Sweden, W.Germany
1990   (Norwich.C) v Finland, Holland, W.Germany, Republic of Ireland, Sweden
1991 v Denmark, Belgium, Iceland, Poland, Germany
1992 v Luxembourg, Republic of Ireland, Austria, Romania, Holland, Argentina, Japan
1993 v Faeroe Islands(2) Cyprus, Belgium(2), Republic of Ireland, Czechoslovakia
1994   (Nottingham.F) v Czechoslovakia, Cyprus, Romania, Norway, Sweden, Estonia
1995 v Albania, Moldova, Germany(2), Bulgaria(2), Greece
1996 v Moldova, Albania

Wegberg, Germany may seem an unusual birthplace for a Welsh international but in the case of David Phillips it does not mean that the Welsh selectors were desperately seeking a player with any kind of national qualification but that the young Phillips first saw the world in Germany because his Caerphilly-born father was stationed there with the RAF. After a few months living in Germany, he lived in Bridgend and

Cardington before moving to Holland when he was nine years old. He was educated at Brunssum and Cornwall and excelled at athletics, rugby and gymnastics. He was the Under-12 British Forces javelin champion and after playing rugby for Wadebridge and St Agnes, won representative honours for Cornwall.

Phillips joined Plymouth Argyle in 1981 as an apprentice and had his baptism in League football in the 1981-82 season, first as a substitute and later as a first-choice midfield player. He established himself in the Home Park club's side the following season but really made his mark in 1983-84 during Argyle's run to the FA Cup semi-finals where they lost to Watford. His performances which included him scoring the goal that won the quarter-final match against Derby County, direct from a corner-kick in injury-time, led to him being selected for three games at Under-21 level in 1984 when he did enough to convince the national selectors that he was ready for senior honours.

Phillips won the first of his 62 full caps for Wales in May 1984 when he gave an outstanding display at full-back - not his normal position in the 1-0 win over England at Wrexham's Racecourse Ground.

Phillips left Plymouth in the summer of 1984 after playing in 93 first team games to join Manchester City for £65,000 plus £15,000 after twenty-five appearances, another £20,000 after fifty appearances and a further £20,000 should he score 20 goals. Though he didn't score 20 goals, he helped the Maine Road club win promotion in 1984-85 when he was ever-present and missed only a few matches in 1985-86 before moving to Coventry City in exchange for goalkeeper Perry Suckling.

Phillips had an outstanding game for Wales against Scotland's Graeme Souness in the World Cup qualifying match at Hampden Park in March 1985 which Wales won 1-0 but six months later he was controversially adjudged to have handled the ball and the subsequent penalty was converted to give the Scots a draw.

In his first season with the Sky Blues, Phillips won an FA Cup winners' medal following Coventry's 3-2 victory over Tottenham Hotspur at Wembley. After three seasons at Highfield Road in which he made 123 appearances, he was allowed to join Norwich City for £525,000, a figure fixed by a tribunal. He marked his debut for the Canaries in a 2-0 win at Sheffield

David Phillips

Wednesday on the opening day of the 1989-90 season with a goal after three minutes and was ever-present in both that campaign and 1990-91. Phillips had scored 20 goals in 186 games for Norwich when, after failing to agree terms for a new contract, he joined Nottingham Forest.

His decision to join the City Ground club was a good one, as his side gained promotion to the Premier League behind Crystal Palace. Over the next couple of seasons, Phillips showed his versatility by playing in midfield and deputising for both full-backs. Still a regular for Wales, his defence-splitting passes and coolness on the ball made him a great favourite with the Forest fans. He had played in 159 games for Forest when a free transfer to Huddersfield Town gave him a new lease of life.

His energy-packed performances brought a touch of class to the Terriers' first team before he was struck down with a troublesome toe problem that put him out of action for the first two months of the 1998-99 season.

A decision was then made to release Phillips in order for him to eventually take on a coaching role and he joined Lincoln City where at the age of thirty-six he has still maintained his enthusiasm and passion for the game.

LEIGHTON PHILLIPS

Birthplace   Briton Ferry
Born   26 September 1949

Football League Career

	Appearances	Goals
Cardiff City	169(11)	11
Aston Villa	134(6)	4
Swansea City	97	0
Charlton Athletic	45	1
Exeter City	10	0

58 caps:
1971   (Cardiff.C) v Czechoslovakia, Scotland, England, N.Ireland
1972 v Czechoslovakia, Romania, Scotland, N.Ireland
1973 v England
1974 v Poland, N.Ireland
1975 v Austria (Aston Villa) v Hungary(2), Luxembourg(2), Scotland, England, N.Ireland
1976 v Austria, England(2) Yugoslavia(2) N.Ireland
1977 v W.Germany, Scotland(2) Czechoslovakia, England
1978 v Kuwait(2) Scotland(2) Czechoslovakia, W.Germany, England
1979 v Malta (Swansea.C) v Turkey, W.Germany, Scotland, England, N.Ireland, Malta
1980 v Republic of Ireland, W.Germany, Turkey, Scotland, N.Ireland, Iceland
1981 v Turkey(2) Czechoslovakia, Scotland, England, USSR
1982   (Charlton.A) v Czechoslovakia 1982

Leighton Phillips always harboured the ambition of becoming a professional football player and after winning Welsh Schoolboy international honours, joined the groundstaff of Cardiff City.

After working his way through the Ninian Park club's ranks, he made his Football League debut as a substitute in a 2-2 draw at home to Rotherham United in January 1968. He scored with his first touch of the ball to draw City level after they had been two goals down. Though he played in a handful of games over the next few seasons, it was 1970-71 before he established himself in the Bluebirds' first team.

At Ninian Park, Phillips had plenty of opportunities to show his versatility, appearing as striker, defender and in midfield before succeeding Brian Harris in the role of sweeper. His performances led to him winning Welsh Under-21 and Under-23 caps before he won the first of his 58 full caps, playing against Czechoslovakia in 1971.

In September 1974 after having appeared in 216 first team games for the Bluebirds, he became dissatisfied at Cardiff's lack of success and left to play for Aston Villa, who paid £80,000 for his services.

Making his debut for Villa as a substitute in a 3-0 win over Millwall,

Leighton Phillips

Phillips went on to captain the club and help them win promotion to the First Division in his first season at Villa Park. He won a League Cup winners' tankard in 1977 as Villa beat Everton, forming an excellent defensive partnership with Chris Nicholl. In fact, it was around this time that Phillips was rated 'the best covering centre-half in the country'. Phillips, who read the game brilliantly, did most most of his best work off the ball, anticipating dangerous situations. A defender of real pace and determination, Phillips returned to South Wales in November 1978 to join Swansea City, after appearing in 175 League and Cup games for the Villans.

Phillips, who cost £70,000, became the Swans' record signing and after making his debut in a 1-0 home win over Bury, he went on to help the Vetch Field club win promotion to the Second Division in his first season with the club. By the time he left Swansea to Join Charlton Athletic in 1981 for a modest £25,000, he had helped the club into the top flight.

His stay at the Valley was brief because the versatile international was beset with injury problems. His last season in the first-class game was 1982-83 when he played as a non-contract player for Exeter City.

Since hanging up his boots, Leighton Phillips has worked for Confederation Life Insurance Company and is now a senior life underwriter for the company.

KEVIN RATCLIFFE

Birthplace   Mancot, Flintshire
Born   12 November 1960

Football League Career

	Appearances	Goals
Everton	356(3)	2
Cardiff City	25	1
Derby County	6	0
Chester City	23	0

59 caps:
1981   (Everton) v Czechoslovakia, Republic of Ireland, Turkey, Scotland, England, USSR
1982 v Czechoslovakia, Iceland, USSR, Spain, England
1983 v Yugoslavia, England, Bulgaria, Scotland, N.Ireland, Brazil
1984 v Norway(2) Romania, Bulgaria, Yugoslavia,Scotland, England, N.Ireland, Israel
1985 v Spain(2) Iceland(2) Norway, Scotland
1986 v Scotland, Hungary, Saudi Arabia, Uruguay
1987 v Finland(2) USSR, Czechoslovakia
1988 v Denmark(2) Czechoslovakia
1989 v Finland, Israel, Sweden, W.Germany
1990 v Finland
1991 v Denmark, Belgium(2), Republic of Ireland, Luxembourg, Iceland, Poland, Germany
1993 v Brazil, Germany, (Cardiff City) v Belgium

The most successful captain in Everton's history, Kevin Ratcliffe played in the same Flintshire schools side as Ian Rush. They grew up together and could have gone to Chester together as apprentices. Rush chose Chester as the launching pad for his career and though a number of top clubs offered Ratcliffe apprentice forms, only one club interested him and that was the team he had supported as a schoolboy, Everton. For on the rare occasions he was not kicking a ball about as a boy, he could be found cheering on the likes of Ball and Royle from the Goodison terraces.

He signed professional forms in 1978 but after kicking his heels in the club's reserve side for two years, he made his Football League debut against Manchester United in March 1980. Despite managing to subdue the fearsome Joe Jordan in a goalless draw, Ratcliffe spent the next two seasons in and out of the Everton side. When he did play, most of his games were at left-back. Ratcliffe was upset by such apparent lack of recognition and by being played out of position, so he went to confront new manager Howard Kendall. At one stage, there was even talk of a move to Ipswich Town when Bobby Robson showed an interest.

During these turbulent times, Ratcliffe, who had won recognition for

Kevin Ratcliffe

Wales at Under-21 level, made his full international debut for Wales against Czechoslovakia, marking dangerman Masny out of the game.

In December 1982, Ratcliffe's fortunes took a decisive upturn when he replaced the overweight Billy Wright alongside Mark Higgins in the heart of the Everton defence. Within twelve months he had succeeded the injury-ravaged Higgins as captain and the following March he was leading his country. After that, Ratcliffe became the calming influence in both the Everton and Wales teams. His role in the Everton side whose game was built on a very sound defensive system, was crucial. The Blues often played a tight and rigid offside game but if a striker did break through, Ratcliffe's speed was such that the danger was snuffed out immediately. Strong in the tackle, Ratcliffe possessed quite a ruthless streak that meant he couldn't be intimidated !

In May 1984, Ratcliffe at the age of 23 became the youngest man since Bobby Moore some twenty years earlier to receive the FA Cup after Watford had been beaten 2-0. He also played in the League Cup Final against Liverpool - and Rush - but this time finished on the losing side. And having been threatened with relegation at Christmas, Everton ended the season in seventh place.

Within the next year, he had led the Blues forward to pick up the FA Charity Shield, the League Championship and the European Cup Winners' Cup in Rotterdam after a 3-1 win over Rapid Vienna. Thereafter he skippered Everton to the runners-up spot in both the League and FA Cup in 1985-86 and to another League title in 1986-87.

In April 1987, Ratcliffe reached another professional milestone in captaining Wales against Czechoslovakia - his fortieth international cap, so beating Everton's previous club record of 39 caps set by England's Alan Ball.

Ratcliffe could read the game with instinctive shrewdness and could close down opponents instantly in moments of danger, often averting crises by clever positional play. Despite losing some of his astonishing speed, he continued to retain the style and consistency that made him one of the world's classiest defenders. During the 1990-91 season, he lost his place to the fast-emerging Martin Keown and in January 1992 he was placed on the transfer list.

In the spring of 1992, after playing in 461 League and Cup games for the Blues, he joined Cardiff City and helped them win promotion to the new Second Division. In April 1995 he was appointed manager of Chester City and in his first two seasons with the club came close to taking them to promotion to the Second Division. Now manager of Shrewsbury Town, Kevin Ratcliffe is one of Goodison Park's most revered sons.

PETER RODRIGUES

Birthplace   Cardiff
Born   21 April 1944

Football League Career

	Appearances	Goals
Cardiff City	85	2
Leicester City	139(1)	6
Sheffield Wednesday	162	2
Southampton	59	3

40 caps:
1965   (Cardiff.C) v N.Ireland, Greece(2)
1966   (Leicester.C) v England, USSR, Scotland, Denmark, N.Ireland, Brazil(2) Chile
1967 v Scotland
1968 v England, Scotland, N.Ireland
1970 v England N.Ireland, E.Germany, Rest of UK
1971   (Sheffield.W) v Romania, England, Scotland, Czechoslovakia, N.Ireland
1972 v Finland, Czechoslovakia, Romania, England, N.Ireland
1973 v England(3), Poland, Scotland, N.Ireland
1974 v Poland

A former Welsh Schoolboy and Youth international, full-back Peter Rodrigues was introduced to League football by his home-town club Cardiff City, though he was very nearly transferred to Newport County for £500 before making his league debut. That came in a 3-3 draw at Sunderland in September 1963, a match in which Ivor Allchurch scored a hat-trick for the Bluebirds. Three months after his league debut, he gained the first of five Under-23 caps for Wales. A fast, attacking full-back, Rodrigues enjoyed nothing more than mounting spectacular overlapping raids down the wing. Particularly quick in recovery, Rodrigues was a virtual ever-present in the Cardiff side for the next few seasons, appearing in both full-back positions. However, the Ninian Park club were unable to offer him the standard of football he required and in December 1965, Rodrigues, who had won the first of forty Welsh caps against Northern Ireland earlier that year, was sold to Leicester City for £42,500, a club record fee.

At Filbert Street, his pace, overlapping inclinations and his ability as the undisputed master of the sliding tackle, brought a new dimension to received notions of full-backs at the Midlands club. His career with the Foxes would surely have stretched much further had it not been for the emergence of Steve Whitworth. Only one disappointing incident - a missed close-range good chance in the 1969 FA Cup Final defeat by Manchester City - remotely overshadowed his stay at Leicester. But as we shall see, he firmly obliterated that particular Wembley memory later in his career. Rodrigues left Filbert Street in October 1970 when Danny Williams paid £50,000 to take him to Sheffield Wednesday.

The Owls, who had just been relegated to the Second Division had started badly and Williams hoped that Rodrigues' arrival would help to turn the tide. In the event, Williams survived in office for only three more months whilst Rodrigues remained to serve two more successors, Dooley and Burtenshaw. However, although Rodrigues held his form and won 17 more caps to his collection whilst at Hillsborough, he was unable to halt the Yorkshire club's gradual slide. After being released on a free transfer in the summer of 1975, Rodrigues' lengthy and distinguished career climaxed in remarkable fashion.

He probably felt that he had achieved all he could in the game when he joined Lawrie McMenemy's Southampton, yet twelve months later, he captained the unfancied south coast club to a shock FA Cup Final win over Manchester United.

Retiring from the game in 1977, Rodrigues kept a public house on the outskirts of the New Forest and at one time coached such local outfits as Telephone Sports, Braishfield, Romsey Town and Blackfield and Langley. He also had a coaching stint in San Diego. In December 1988, Rodrigues returned to Wales to become landlord of a pub in Carmarthen. He now works in a local conservative club, whilst still being actively involved in running and promoting the Tenby Soccer Schools.

LEIGH ROOSE

Birthplace   Holt, nr Wrexham
Born   27 November 1877
Died   7 October 1916

Football League Career

	Appearances	Goals
Stoke City	146	0
Everton	18	0
Sunderland	92	0
Huddersfield Town	5	0
Aston Villa	10	0
Arsenal	13	0

24 caps:
1900   (Aberystwyth.T) v Ireland
1901   (London Welsh) v Scotland, England, Ireland
1902   (Stoke) v England, Scotland
1904 v England
1905   (Everton) v Scotland, England
1906   (Stoke) v Scotland, England, Ireland
1907 v Ireland, Scotland, England
1908   (Sunderland) v Scotland, England
1909 v Scotland, England, Ireland
1910 v Scotland, England, Ireland
1911 v Scotland

Leigh Richmond Roose was one of the most famous amateur players of the pre-World War One period. The son of a Presbyterian minister, he was educated at the Holt Academy where he was taught by H.G.Wells. After taking a Science degree at Aberystwyth University, he began his football career with the town's club, his performances winning him the first of 24 caps for Wales when he played against Ireland at Llandudno on 24 February 1900. A crowd of 6,000 saw Wales win 2-0 with Billy Meredith clinching victory with a late penalty. Whilst with Aberystwyth, he helped them win the Welsh Cup but later moved to Ruabon Druids.

Roose moved to King's College Hospital, London to train as a doctor but despite taking a keen interest in bacteriology, he never qualified and remained an enthusiastic student !

In October 1901, Roose joined Stoke as an amateur, though he proved to be a very expensive player to have, because he paid little attention to the rules which his professional colleagues in the team had to obey. As he lived in London, Roose was faced with a long journey most Saturdays and if the normal train service did not suit his requirements, he would hire a special train for himself before arriving at the ground in a hansom cab! Wherever he played, his mere presence on the team sheet would add thousands to the attendance, so individual was his style, so powerful his personality.

In November 1904, Roose joined Everton and though his stay was brief, he played his part in the club's progress to the FA Cup semi-final and the runners-up spot in the First Division. At the end of the season he rejoined Stoke and took his total of League appearances to 146 before moving to Sunderland.

In recognition of his services to the Wearsiders, when a series of outstanding displays helped save the club from relegation, the Sunderland board were eager to give Roose a testimonial match. The FA decided that this was not feasible due to Roose's amateur status and he had to make do with an illuminated address from the Mayor.

'Dick' Roose could punch the ball further than most players could kick it and although on occasions his genius proved erratic, it was compelling. In the match against Scotland at Kilmarnock in March 1910, he stretched half-heartedly for a 40-yard shot from Falkirk's Andrew Divine and missed it completely to gift Scotland the only goal of the game !

As an amateur, Roose played for a variety of clubs and signed for different sides at different times for different leagues. This led to one of the most famous incidents in the history of the Potteries derby matches between Stoke City and Port Vale. It was on 23 April 1910 and Port Vale were visiting the Victoria Ground for a game that would decide the championship of the North Staffordshire and District League against Stoke Reserves. After a glut of fixtures, Port Vale's committee decided to take no chances and signed four notable amateurs for this final game to bolster their chances. Roose was one of these four. Vale were leading 2-0 and the Stoke crowd could take no more, rejecting these dubious tactics, they stormed the pitch, carrying Roose towards the River Trent for a ducking. Stoke chairman Revd A.E.Hurst ran on to the pitch to appeal for calm and the Stoke forward Horrocks was knocked out in the melee before Roose was released with the help of police ! Roose who had performed brilliantly said he believed the game was only a friendly and did not realise a championship was at stake !

Roose was also a great practical joker. Railway personnel were especially wary of him after so many of them had been asked to go and feed his dog in the guard's van. Off they would go with their hands cupped full of biscuits only to find no dog and no sign of Roose either when the railwaymen went back up the train in search of him !

He also once turned up for an international match in Belfast with his hand heavily bandaged, telling everyone not to worry, that he'd only broken a couple of bones but would be able to play. The photographers crowded around the Welsh goal just before the start of play but once play was in progress, Roose calmly unwound the bandage and went on to perform heroics in a 3-2 win.

The Welsh international 'keeper was also a most generous individual and once offered to stand down from the Wales team to allow Alf Edwards, who had been named as reserve on eight occasions, the opportunity to make his debut. Sadly, the Welsh selectors were not of the same opinion.

Roose's playing days were approaching their end when he joined the 9th Battalion Royal Fusiliers on the outbreak of the First World War. Lance Corporal Roose, who was awarded the Military Medal was reputedly last seen on the battlefield by Gordon Hoare, the England Amateur international and officially lost on 7 October 1916.

IAN RUSH

Birthplace   St Asaph
Born   20 October 1961

Football League Career

	Appearances	Goals
Chester City	33(1)	14
Liverpool	447(22)	229
Leeds United	34(2)	3
Newcastle United	6(4)	0
Sheffield United	4	0
Wrexham	12(5)	0

73 caps: 28 goals.
1980   (Liverpool) v Scotland, N.Ireland
1981 v England
1982 v USSR, Iceland, England, Sweden, N.Ireland, France
1983 v Norway, Yugoslavia, England, Bulgaria
1984 v Norway, Bulgaria, Romania, Yugoslavia, Scotland, England, N.Ireland
1985 v Iceland, Norway, Scotland, Spain
1986 v Scotland, Saudi Arabia, Republic of Ireland, Uruguay
1987 v Finland(2) USSR, Czechoslovakia
1988   (Juventus) v Denmark, Czechoslovakia, Yugoslavia, Sweden, Malta, Italy
1989   (Liverpool) v Holland, Finland, Sweden, W.Germany
1990 v Finland, Republic of Ireland
1991 v Denmark, Belgium(2) Luxembourg, Republic of Ireland, Poland, W.Germany
1992 v Germany, Luxembourg, Romania
1993 v Faeroe Islands(2) Cyprus, Belgium(2) Czechoslovakia
1994 v Czechoslovakia, Cyprus, Romania, Norway, Sweden, Estonia
1995 v Albania, Georgia(2), Bulgaria, Greece
1996 v Moldova, Italy

One of ten children - seven of them boys, Ian Rush began his career with Chester. At Sealand Road, the schoolboy international was used mostly in midfield but his goalscoring abilities had already been spotted by Liverpool representatives. Although chased by the Anfield club, Rush had a preference for Everton, whom he supported as a boy or Manchester City, where he felt he would have a better chance of first team football.

Bob Paisley paid £300,000 for the youngster in April 1980. Many doubted the shrewdness of this acquisition and in his early days at Anfield, he could hardly find the net in Central League games - there was even talk of him moving on. Liverpool took care not to rush Rush !

He became a full international over six months before his first team debut, first as a substitute in the 1-0 defeat by Scotland on 21 My 1980, then as a full cap against Northern Ireland at Ninian Park. His first goal for Wales came in May 1982 against the Irish at Wrexham. By this time, he had become a firm favourite of the Kop.

In the 1981-82 season, he scored 30 goals in 49 games, to win his first League Championship medal, including one on his first appearance in the Merseyside derby as Liverpool beat Everton 3-1.

His best individual performance in the derby game came exactly a year later in Liverpool's 5-0 humiliation of the old enemy at Goodison - his four goal haul being only the third time this feat had been achieved. Rush's goals record in the derbies is unparalleled, his total of 21 being the best of either side. There were further League titles in 1982-83 and 1983-84, European Cup victory in 1984 and League Cup wins in 1983 and 1984.

His impact on the FA Cup competition was immediate, scoring on his debut for Chester in their 5-1 drubbing of Workington in the first round in November 1979. He scored two FA Cup hat-tricks, in March 1985 when Liverpool beat Barnsley 4-0 at Oakwell and then in 1989 when Liverpool thrashed Swansea City 8-0 at Anfield.

Unlike some run-of-the-mill strikers, Ian Rush was the focal point of the Liverpool attacks, collecting the ball out of defence and laying it off simply but effectively before speeding off to a new position. The sight of him breaking free to leave defenders in his wake before slotting home the ball is one that will linger long in the memory.

Ian Rush

Perhaps the peak of his career was 1985-86 when the Reds lifted the near-impossible League and Cup double. His 23 goals were crucial in helping Liverpool to win the First Division title for a record sixteenth time, whilst he also scored twice in the 3-1 FA Cup Final victory over Everton.

Liverpool's dependence on Rush's flow of goals was shown by the run of 144 matches in which the side never lost when Ian scored. That record was broken when his 202nd goal was overtaken by two by Charlie Nicholas as Arsenal won the 1987 Littlewoods Cup Final.

Rush's reputation as one of the world's most feared strikers had clubs battling for his signature. Juventus succeeded in a deal worth £3.2 million. There was one consolation for the Anfield faithful in that he would be staying for one more season. Rush showed his greatness by playing his heart out and scoring 30 goals in 42 League games. He ended the season in style, hitting two goals in a 3-1 win over Everton and the winner in the final game at Anfield against Watford before throwing his shirt to the Kop.

The move to Juventus, where he had to come to terms with the man-to-man marking of the Italian game, provided him with a fresh and intriguing challenge - and financial security for life ! Sadly, however, after the retirement of former French captain Michel Platini, Rush no longer received the service that he needed. Goals were sparse and Rush came under increasing pressure from the voracious Italian media as he tried to justify the huge transfer fee.

On the eve of the 1988-89 season, Liverpool manager Kenny Dalglish surprised the soccer world by paying £2.8 million to bring Rush back to Anfield. Intriguingly he was for some while both Liverpool's record sale and record purchase.

Though he took some time to readjust after being troubled by illness and injuries, Rush proved his worth by coming on as a substitute in the 1989 FA Cup Final and scoring two opportunist goals to help beat Everton. During the 1992-93 season, Rush broke Roger Hunt's record haul of 286 goals for the club with his first-ever goal against Manchester United and his first in the Premier League. Although the goals were never as regular as they once were, Rush continued to terrify defences throughout the Football League before his transfer to Leeds United in May 1996.

Although the writing had been on the wall when Liverpool signed Stan

Collymore, Ian won his first team place back following Collymore's indifferent early season performances and only lost it through injury. Happily he signed off his Anfield career with a goal in his last Premiership match for the club at Manchester City to bring his total to 346 in 659 games for the Anfield club.

At Elland Road he hit the worst goalscoring drought of his long career, going fifteen games without finding the net and in the close season he joined Newcastle United. Although only expecting to be used as a squad player, the club's early season striker crisis, led to him playing more often than he expected. His first goal for the Magpies came in the League Cup against Hull City, taking his career total to 49 and equalling Geoff Hurst's competition record. He also helped Newcastle on their way to Wembley with the FA Cup third round winner against old rivals Everton, extending his record as the top FA Cup goalscorer this century with 43 goals.

Released in the summer, he joined Wrexham as player-coach. Capped by Wales on 73 occasions, the goalscoring legend continued to struggle with injuries and after passing on his vast experience to the Racecourse youngsters, he left the club in the summer of 1999.

DEAN SAUNDERS

Birthplace   Swansea
Born   21 June 1964

Football League Career

	Appearances	Goals
Swansea City	42(7)	12
Cardiff City	3(1)	0
Brighton and Hove Albion	66(6)	21
Oxford United	57(2)	22
Derby County	106	42
Liverpool	42	11
Aston Villa	111(1)	37
Nottingham Forest	39(4)	5

69 caps: 21 goals.
1986   (Brighton.HA) v Republic of Ireland, Canada(2)
1987 v Finland, USSR
1988   (Oxford.U) v Yugoslavia, Sweden, Malta, Italy
1989 v Holland (Derby.C) v Finland, Israel, Sweden, W.Germany
1990 v Finland, Holland, W.Germany, Sweden, Costa Rica
1991 v Denmark, Belgium(2) Luxembourg, Republic of Ireland, Iceland, Poland, W.Germany
1992   (Liverpool) v Brazil, Germany, Republic of Ireland, Romania, Holland, Argentina, Japan
1993 v Faeroe Islands (Aston Villa) v Cyprus, Belgium(2) Czechoslovakia, Faeroe Islands
1994 v Czechoslovakia, Cyprus, Romania, Norway,
1995 v Georgia(2) Bulgaria(2) Germany
1996   (Galatasaray) v Germany, Albania, San Marino
1997   (Nottingham.F)v San Marino, Holland(2) Turkey, Belgium, Scotland
1998 v Turkey, Belgium, Brazil (Sheffield.U) v Malta Tunisia
1999 v Italy, Denmark, Belarus (Benfica) v Switzerland, Italy, Denmark

The son of Roy who played for Liverpool and Swansea City, Dean Saunders was thrown into League action in October 1983 with the Swans just relegated from Division One. With Swansea struggling, Saunders was an ever-present for the last fifteen matches but could not prevent them dropping into Division Three. With John Bond taking over from Colin Appleton in December 1984, top-scorer Saunders was loaned to Second Division Cardiff City. Swansea missed another relegation by one point and Saunders, given a free transfer by Bond, joined Second Division Brighton and Hove Albion.

He quickly justified the Seagulls' confidence, scoring 19 League and Cup goals in a side that was in the top half of Division Two and reached the FA Cup fifth round. His form convinced Wales' manager Mike England to include him in the squad for the close season tour of Canada,

Saunders having made his international debut against the Republic of Ireland in Dublin a few weeks earlier. The 1986-87 season didn't go as well for Saunders and he had only scored seven goals when the hard up south coast club accepted a bid of £60,000 from Oxford United.

His six goals in the last twelve matches included two vital ones at Kenilworth Road when Oxford United secured their First Division status in the penultimate game of the season. The 1987-88 season was particularly successful for Saunders, whose 21 goals included six in the League Cup and helped United to a second semi-final in three seasons. His blistering pace and spectacular reflex shooting were accompanied by much chanting of his nickname 'Deano'. It was whilst he was at the Manor Ground that Saunders, despite the presence of Mark Hughes and Ian Rush, began to establish himself as a regular in the Welsh side.

On 22 October 1988, Saunders was transferred to Derby County for £1 million, the repercussions of which led to an angry Mark Lawrenson being sacked as manager.

Saunders immediately set about repaying the massive fee with some spectacular goals for both the Rams and Wales, thus dispelling any lingering doubts about the inflated fee. In those seasons at the Baseball Ground, he was Derby's leading scorer with a best of 17 from just 37 scored in 1990-91. During the close season he moved to Liverpool for £2.9 million, a record transfer between two English clubs.

Unfortunately he never really showed his usual sharpness at Anfield. Coming into a Liverpool side undergoing radical changes and hit by injury, he never received the kind of service he needed as Liverpool continued to play a very different game to the one that Saunders excelled in. In September 1992 he was sold to Aston Villa for £2.3 million and his career was suddenly resurrected. After making his debut at Leeds United, he played in every other game in that 1992-93 season, finishing as leading scorer with 17 goals as Villa ended the campaign as runners-up in the Premier League to Manchester United. He was top scorer in 1993-94 with ten goals including a hat-trick against Swindon Town and in 1994-95 with 15 goals. At the end of that season he joined Turkish club Galatasaray before returning to the Premiership with Nottingham Forest.

Though he didn't have the best of times at the City Ground, he retained

Dean Saunders

his place in the Welsh side and scored in the World Cup qualifiers. Eventually he was allowed to move to Sheffield United on a free transfer for whom he scored one of the best goals of the 1997-98 season, volleying past the Port Vale 'keeper from the touchline. His form for the Blades was outstanding and not surprisingly he added to his total of Welsh caps. However, due to a clause in his contract, the Yorkshire club were powerless to prevent his move to Benfica for £500,000 in December 1998.

In the summer of 1999, Saunders returned to Yorkshire to play for Premiership new boys Bradford City, where even at the age of thirty-five, he has managed to get in behind defenders and hurt them with his pace.

ALF SHERWOOD

Birthplace	Aberaman
Born	13 November 1923
Died	12 March 1990

Football League Career

	Appearances	Goals
Cardiff City	353	15
Newport County	205	21

41 caps:
1947   (Cardiff.C) v England, N.Ireland
1948 v Scotland, N.Ireland
1949 v England, Scotland, N.Ireland, Portugal, Switzerland
1950 v England, Scotland, N.Ireland, Belgium
1951 v England, Scotland, N.Ireland, Portugal, Switzerland
1952 v England, Scotland, N.Ireland, Rest of UK
1953 v Scotland, England, N.Ireland, France, Yugoslavia
1954 v England, Scotland, N.Ireland, Austria
1955 v Scotland, England, Yugoslavia, N.Ireland
1956 v England, Scotland, N.Ireland, Austria
1957   (Newport.C) v England, Scotland

A master of the sliding tackle, Alf Sherwood's pace, tackling ability and positional sense made him one of the best full-backs in the Football League and the one defender who could subdue the great Stanley Matthews.

Sherwood played for his home-town team Aberaman, playing alongside war-time 'guests' such as Dai Astley and Bryn Jones. He had gained Welsh schoolboy honours at both soccer and cricket, appearing in the same side as Trevor Ford and Gilbert Parkhouse, the latter going on to play for Glamorgan and England as an opening batsman.

Sherwood played his early football as a wing-half and it was in that position that he first came to Cardiff City's attention. He was playing against the Bluebirds in a War League game at Ninian Park and was so impressive that City manager Cyril Spiers signed him there and then. That was in 1941 and over the next few years of wartime football, he turned out whenever he could get away from working down the pits. During a game against Lovells Athletic, Cardiff found themselves short at the back. Sherwood agreed to have a go and after performing as if he'd always played in this position, he stayed there for the rest of his career.

Sherwood who played in 140 wartime games for Cardiff, made his Football League debut in a 2-1 defeat at Norwich City on the opening day of the 1946-47 season. Missing just one game, he helped the Bluebirds win the Third Division (South) Championship that campaign as they finished nine points ahead of runners-up Queen's Park Rangers.

Sherwood, who had played in an earlier Victory international against Ireland, was given his full cap for Wales when he was selected to play against England at Maine Road in October 1946. Though his full-back partner in that match was captain Billy Hughes of Birmingham, it was Arsenal's Walley Barnes who was to become his partner for the next six years of international football.

Following Fred Stansfield's departure to Newport County, where he later became manager, Sherwood's defensive partner at Ninian Park was Ron Stitfall. Sherwood was appointed the Bluebirds' captain and in 1951-52 led the side into the top flight after finishing runners-up in the Second Division to Sheffield Wednesday.

He was also the stand-in goalkeeper for both Cardiff City and Wales.

When the Bluebirds travelled to Anfield for an end of season game in April 1954, the home side had to win to keep their First Division status. City were 1-0 up when Sherwood, who had taken over in goal from the injured Ron Howells had to face a penalty from Liverpool's Scottish international winger Billy Liddell. He saved it and Liverpool were relegated ! For Wales he had replaced the injured Jack Kelsey in the match against England at Wembley in November 1956. Once again he produced a series of magnificent saves but Wales lost 3-1.

Sherwood had appeared in 383 League and Cup games for Cardiff City when it became apparent that he was no longer part of manager Trevor Morris' plans. He left Ninian Park in the summer of 1956 to join Newport County where he confounded his critics by not only playing in 205 games for the Somerton Park club but by also winning two more caps for Wales to take his total to 41.

His international career had spanned ten years and saw him captain Wales on a number of occasions including the famous 2-1 win over England at Ninian Park in 1955.

In the early 1960s, Sherwood spent three summers in New York in an attempt to promote the game in the United States. On his return to the British Isles he had a brief spell as manager of Barry Town but after ending his involvement with the game, he worked in insurance before being employed as a security officer with the National Coal Board.

NEVILLE SOUTHALL

Birthplace   Llandudno
Born   16 September 1958

Football League Career

	Appearances	Goals
Bury	39	0
Everton	578	0
Port Vale	9	0
Southend United	9	0

Stoke City	12	0
Torquay United	25	0
Bradford City	1	0

92 caps:
1982   (Everton) v N.Ireland
1983 v Norway, England, Bulgaria, Scotland, N.Ireland, Brazil
1984 v Norway, Romania, Bulgaria,Yugoslavia, Scotland, England, N.Ireland, Norway, Israel
1985 v Iceland(2) Spain(2) Norway(2) Scotland
1986 v Scotland, Hungary, Saudi Arabia, Republic of Ireland
1987 v USSR, Finland Czechoslovakia
1988 v Denmark, Czechoslovakia, Yugoslavia, Sweden
1989 v Holland, Finland, Sweden, W.Germany
1990 v Finland, Holland, W.Germany, Republic of Ireland, Sweden, Costa Rica
1991 v Denmark, Belgium(2) Luxembourg, Republic of Ireland, Iceland, Poland, W.Germany
1992 v Brazil, Germany, Luxembourg, Republic of Ireland, Austria, Romania, Holland, Argentina, Japan
1993 v Faeroe Islands(2) Cyprus, Belgium(2), Republic of Ireland, Czechoslovakia
1994 v Czechoslovakia, Cyprus, Romania, Norway, Sweden, Estonia
1995 v Albania, Moldova, Georgia(2) Bulgaria(2) Germany
1996 v Moldova, Germany, Albania, Italy, San Marino
1997 v San Marino, Holland(2), Turkey, Belarus
1998 v Turkey

As a boy Neville Southall played for the Caernarfon District side as a centre-half but after turning out as emergency goalkeeper for Llandudno Swifts against Rhos Aelwyd, he shelved any thoughts about being an outfield player to concentrate on goalkeeping.

Southall was then just 14 years old, making him one of the youngest players to appear in the Welsh League (North). When he left school,

Southall took a job with the local council, demolishing gun emplacements built during the Second World War. After working as a dustman, he found employment at the Ritz Cafe in Llandudno before spending several years working on building sites as a hod carrier.

While living in Llandudno, he kept goal for both Bangor City and Conwy United but it was his fine form for Winsford United that caused Bury to pay £6,000 for him in June 1980. In the summer of 1981, after only 44 first team appearances for the Gigg Lane club, he signed for Everton in a £150,000 deal.

He made his debut for the Blues on 17 October 1981 in a 2-1 win over Ipswich Town. Things didn't go too smoothly for him after that and following a 5 0 home defeat at the hands of rivals Liverpool, Southall was dropped and replaced by former Blackburn Rovers' 'keeper Jim Arnold, while Southall learned his trade.

He was sent on loan to Port Vale but after just nine appearances for the Valiants he was recalled by the Merseyside club. He was ever-present for that and the next two seasons as his form and Everton's improved beyond all expectations.

He had made his international debut for Wales on 27 May 1982, keeping a clean sheet in a 3-0 win over Northern Ireland.

In 1984 he got his first taste of glory when Everton won the FA Cup for the first time in eighteen years, beating Watford 2-0. Two of his saves from John Barnes contributed greatly to the club's victory. The following season, Everton won the League Championship, the European Cup-Winners' Cup and were runners-up in the FA Cup. At the end of the season he became only the fourth goalkeeper to win the Player of the Year award, following in the footsteps of Bert Trautmann, Gordon Banks and Pat Jennings. In fact, the former Spurs, Arsenal and Northern Ireland 'keeper described Southall as 'a 'keeper without a weakness'. One save that season from Mark Falco which effectively ended Spurs' challenge, had experienced writers going back to Gordon Banks' famous save from Pele in the 1970 World Cup for a comparison. His colleagues though were more blasé, saying that 'Nev' made saves like that every week !

Southall frequently produced saves that proved to be the turning point of crucial matches. His anticipation was superb and he was an excellent

Neville Southall

shot-stopper but what gave him the edge was an astonishing capacity to change direction at the last moment, sometimes even in mid-air and an instinct for improvising unorthodox saves. Southall also displayed great courage on countless occasions, diving in amid a mass of boots to catch low crosses.

He suffered severe dislocation of the ankle and ligament damage playing for Wales against the Republic of Ireland in March 1986. The injury was so acute that it was wondered if he would ever be able to get back to his brilliant best. He recovered in time to collect his second League Championship medal as Everton won the title again in 1987. His world class performances played a major part in Everton's rise to one of England's top clubs.

His part in one bizarre incident - a goalmouth sit-in after walking out of a half-time harangue by Everton manager Colin Harvey - did the big Welshman less than credit, even though Southall is his own man and was acting out of frustration rather than malice.

Time finally began to catch up with the Welsh goalkeeping wizard midway through the 1996-97 season. He made a record breaking 700th first team appearance for the Blues on the opening day of the season, received an MBE from the Queen in the Birthday Honours list but then found himself dropped for the first time in fifteen years after the FA Cup upset against Bradford City. However, the following season saw Southall establish new records at Goodison. Having become the first footballer to appear in 200 Premiership matches, he made his 750th appearance in an Everton jersey, a figure never likely to be matched.

After a loan spell with Southend United he joined Stoke City, also on loan before the move became permanent. Freed by the Potters in the summer of 1998, the vastly experienced 'keeper played non-League football for Doncaster Rovers before returning to League action with Torquay United. After just 27 appearances, he walked away with the Gulls' Player of the Year award. In March 2000, Southall returned to the Premiership for Bradford City but was on the losing side in a 2-1 home defeat by Leeds United.

As his Welsh team-mate and former Liverpool centre-forward Ian Rush said 'For sheer consistency, there's no-one to touch Neville.'

GARY SPEED

Birthplace Hawarden
Born   8 September 1969

Football League Career

	Appearances	Goals
Leeds United	231(17)	39
Everton	58	15
Newcastle United	47(4)	5

52 caps: 3 goals.
1990   (Leeds.U) v Costa Rica
1991 v Denmark, Luxembourg, Republic of Ireland, Iceland, W.Germany
1992 v Brazil, Germany, Luxembourg, Republic of Ireland, Romania, Holland, Argentina, Japan
1993 v Faeroe Islands(2) Cyprus, Belgium(2) Republic of Ireland
1994 v Czechoslovakia, Cyprus, Romania, Norway, Sweden
1995 v Albania, Moldova, Georgia, Bulgaria(2) Germany
1996 v Moldova, Germany, Italy, Switzerland
1997   (Everton) v San Marino, Holland(2) Turkey, Republic of Ireland, Belgium, Scotland
1998 v Turkey, Brazil (Newcastle.U) v Jamaica, Malta, Tunisia
1999 v Italy(2) Denmark(2) Switzerland

Joining Leeds United straight from Hawarden Grammar School in 1987, Welsh Youth international Gary Speed earned his chance in the Yorkshire club's first team in May 1989 when he played against Oldham Athletic after scoring in twelve consecutive Northern Intermediate League games.

He started the 1989-90 season on the bench but became a regular in the Championship run-in and scored a memorable goal against Sheffield United following a 60-yard dash with the ball. Speed was called up for Wales in October 1989 as a late replacement to the squad for a World Cup qualifier at Wrexham. On that occasion he sat out the game on the substitute's bench but at the end of the season after helping United to the Second Division title, he made his full international debut. On 19 May 1990, he played for the Wales Under-21 side at Merthyr against Poland and the following day turned out for the full side against Costa Rica. That was the start of a long international career which has seen him win 52 caps to date.

For Leeds, Speed had a truly remarkable League Championship-winning season in 1991-92, when his forays down the left-wing brought him, and others, plenty of goals. Speed, was always one of the first names on Howard Wilkinson's team sheet. Although preferring to play in a more central role, Speed's versatility has allowed him to play in a variety of roles and towards the end of that League Championship-winning season, he replaced Tony Dorigo as the club's left-back. After a couple of lean seasons, Speed looked to have regained all his old consistency and goalscoring ability but towards the end of the 1995-96 season, he suffered a fractured cheek bone against Port Vale but such was his commitment to the Elland Road club that he returned to first team action five weeks later.

It was around this time that Everton made a £3.5 million bid for Speed's services. This was turned down but under three months later, the deal did go through, enabling Speed to join the side he had supported as a youngster when he played for Manchester City's nursery side, Blue Star. In fact, Speed was once a paper boy for former Everton and Wales' captain, Kevin Ratcliffe !

He enjoyed a dream start to his Goodison career, scoring on his debut in a 2-0 win over Newcastle United. He went on to record his best goals return since winning the Championship with Leeds in 1991-92. Included in his total of eleven goals was his first senior hat-trick in the 7-1 defeat of Southampton at Goodison Park. Everton manager Howard Kendall sprang a surprise by naming the influential midfielder as the Blues' new captain for the 1997-98 season. Speed responded with some of the most consistent displays of his career as he found himself employed in a more central midfield role. However, midway through the campaign, there were rumours that he was unhappy at the club he had supported since a boy and the situation came to a head when he refused to travel to West Ham United. Soon after, he was sold to Newcastle United for £5.5 million,

Gary Speed

being prevented from telling his side of the story by signing a non-disclosure agreement.

He ended his first season at St James' Park with a runners-up medal following the Magpies FA Cup Final defeat at the hands of Arsenal. In 1998-99 following David Batty's transfer to Leeds, Speed, who occasionally captained the north-east club, moved into a central midfield role, where he clearly felt more at home. A player with pace, control and notable heading ability, he continues to be a regular in the Welsh side.

GARY SPRAKE

Birthplace   Swansea
Born   3 April 1945

Football League Career
                    Appearances   Goals
Leeds United   381   0
Birmingham City   16   0

37 caps:
1964   (Leeds.U) v Scotland, N.Ireland
1965 v Scotland, Denmark, Greece
1966 v England, USSR, N.Ireland
1967 v Scotland
1968 v England, Scotland
1969 v W.Germany, Scotland, England, N.Ireland
1970 v Rest of UK, E.Germany, Italy
1971 v Romania, Scotland, England, N.Ireland
1972 v Finland, England, Scotland, N.Ireland
1973 v England(2) Poland, Scotland, N.Ireland
1974 v Poland (Birmingham .C) v Scotland, N.Ireland
1975 v Austria, Hungary, Luxembourg

Gary Sprake lived next door but one to Arsenal and Wales goalkeeper Jack Kelsey. Sprake too was capped by his country, becoming the Principality's youngest-ever goalkeeper when he made his debut against Scotland in November 1963, aged 18 years 231 days old. Sprake left school at the age of fifteen to take an apprenticeship as a fitter and turner, playing in goal for the works team. He was spotted by Leeds United's Welsh-based scout Jack Pickard, who also discovered John Charles playing for Swansea Schools.

In March 1962, Sprake made an unexpected first team debut for the Elland Road club. He was enjoying a lie-in when frantic Leeds officials contacted him in the morning of United's Second Division game at Southampton. The club's first-choice 'keeper Tommy Younger had been taken ill and so 16-year-old Sprake was rushed to Manchester's Ringway Airport and flown to the south coast in a two-seater plane for a dramatic league debut. The game kicked-off fifteen minutes late because of United's predicament and although the Saints won 4-1, Sprake had impressed enough and the following season, won Younger's place on merit.

Leeds manager Don Revie thought very highly of Sprake and when the young 'keeper abandoned Elland Road after feeling homesick and losing his confidence, to return to South Wales, Revie followed him to convince the blond-haired six footer that he had a future in the game.

Sprake eventually made the breakthrough into the Leeds first team in September 1962 in the match against Swansea at the Vetch Field, a game the Yorkshire club won 2-0. He was the Leeds first-choice 'keeper for the next ten seasons, during which time he won a League Championship medal, a League Cup winners' medal, two Inter Cities Fairs Cup medals and a Division Two Championship medal.

When Leeds won the League Championship in 1968-69, Sprake was an ever-present as the Elland Road club won the title with the fewest number of goals conceded by any champions. At the start of that season, Sprake produced heroics to keep out Ferencvaros of Hungary and help Leeds secure a goalless draw and so win the Inter Cities Fairs Cup for the first time.

A member of the phenomenal Leeds United side of the 1970s, Sprake played in 507 first team games, more than any other Elland Road goalkeeper. Although Sprake was an acrobatic and exciting 'keeper he was also prone to lapses of concentration, more often than not when the TV cameras were present. One famous Sprake incident came at Anfield where he literally threw the ball into his own net ! Yet in spite of these occasional blunders, Gary Sprake was a goalkeeper of the highest class, winning 37 Welsh caps, 32 of them as a Leeds United player.

On losing his place to David Harvey, Sprake was transferred to Birmingham City in October 1973 for a fee of £100,000. He had made just 16 league appearances for the St Andrew's club when injury and illness forced his premature retirement from the game. Living in Solihull, Sprake briefly worked as a rep for a sports good firm but now works for the local council as a training officer, responsible for placing business trainees and monitoring their progress.

Gary Sprake

DEREK TAPSCOTT

Birthplace   Barry
Born   30 June 1932

Football League Career

	Appearances	Goals
Arsenal	119	62
Cardiff City	194	79
Newport County	12(1)	1

14 caps: 4 goals.
1954   (Arsenal) v Austria
1955 v Scotland, England, N.Ireland, Yugoslavia
1956 v England, N.Ireland, Scotland, Austria
1957 v N.Ireland, Czechoslovakia, E.Germany
1959   (Cardiff.C) v England, N.Ireland

Derek Tapscott was one of the Football League's most consistent goalscorers of the mid and late 1950s. On leaving school, Tapscott, who hailed from a family of 17, had a variety of jobs including working on a building site. He also played football for his home-town side Barry Town in the Welsh and Southern Leagues where he built up a reputation as a prolific goalscorer. During his two years National Service, he was given a game in Tottenham Hotspur's reserve side but nothing came of it, so he returned to South Wales to continue his career with Barry Town.

In October 1953, Arsenal manager Tom Whittaker invited 'Tappy' as he was known to Highbury and gave him the chance to sign for one of the most famous teams in the country. He didn't need asking twice and though he had to take a pay cut from his combined football and building labourer wages, he soon put pen to paper.

Playing for the Gunners' Football Combination side, Tapscott was finding the back of the net with great regularity and was often asked to accompany the first team to games to get him accustomed to the big match atmosphere. Eventually he made his league debut alongside

Tommy Lawton in the match against Liverpool at Highbury towards the end of that 1953-54 season. He celebrated by scoring twice in a 3-0 win but watched sadly as Joe Mercer's career was ended by a broken leg. Three days later, Tapscott was called into the manager's office and told that he had beens elected to win his first cap in the friendly international against Austria. Though the match was classed as a friendly, it was anything but and Tapscott's continual barging of the Austrian goalkeeper had a lot to do with it ! Though it wasn't illegal, barging was not a tactic favoured by continental sides. Tapscott came close to scoring on a number of occasions but the Austrians won 2-0.

On his return to Highbury, he scored twice in a 3-0 win over Portsmouth and ended the season with five goals in as many matches. In 1954-55 he won a regular place in the Arsenal side, scoring 13 goals in 37 games. The following season, Tapscott was the Gunners' leading scorer with 21 goals and in 1956-57 he scored 25 league goals, the most since Ronnie Rooke netted 33 in 1947-48. Early the following season when he seemed to be at his peak, he had to undergo a cartilage operation but sadly when he had regained full fitness, he couldn't find his form of the previous three seasons. In fact the injury and his loss of form cost him his place in the Welsh side for the 1958 World Cup Finals in Sweden.

Arsenal too decided that Tapscott had no future in the top flight and sold him to Cardiff City for a fee of £15,000.

Though he failed to score on his debut for the Bluebirds as they beat Grimsby Town 4-1, he was the club's leading scorer with 20 League goals in 1959-60, as City won promotion to the First Division. He was the club's top scorer again the following season with 21 goals in 39 League games including his first hat-trick for the club as West Bromwich Albion were beaten 3-1.

Despite City being relegated in 1961-62, Tapscott netted his second hat-trick for the club in a 3-2 home win over Birmingham City. He scored his third League hat-trick the following season in a 4-2 win at Charlton Athletic.

Tapscott continued to score on a regular basis and in seven years at Ninian Park, he netted 99 goals in 233 first team games including six in the 16-0 Welsh Cup defeat of Knighton in 1960-61 - still the individual scoring record of any Cardiff player in a first team fixture.

In July 1965 he joined Newport County before later moving into non-League football with Cinderford Town and Carmarthen. After hanging up his boots, he took up the position of a sportswear representative.

MICKEY THOMAS

Birthplace   Mochdre nr Colwyn Bay
Born   7 July 1954

Football League Career

	Appearances	Goals
Wrexham	243(13)	34
Manchester United	90	11
Everton	10	0
Brighton and Hove Albion	18(2)	0
Stoke City	97(6)	21
Chelsea	43(1)	9
West Bromwich Albion	20	0
Derby County	9	0
Shrewsbury Town	40	1
Leeds United	3	0

51 caps: 4 goals.
1977   (Wrexham) v W.Germany, Scotland(2) N.Ireland
1978 v Kuwait, Scotland, Czechoslovakia, Iran, England, N.Ireland
1979 v Malta (Manchester.U) v Turkey, W.Germany, Malta
1980 v Republic of Ireland, W.Germany, Turkey, England, Scotland, N.Ireland
1981 v Czechoslovakia, Scotland, England, USSR
1982   (Everton) v Czechoslovakia (Brighton.HA) v USSR? Spain, England, Scotland, N.Ireland
1983   (Stoke.C) v Norway, Yugoslavia, England, Bulgaria, Scotland, N.Ireland, Brazil

1984 v Romania, Bulgaria, Yugoslavia (Chelsea) v Scotland, England
1985 v N.Ireland, Spain(2) Iceland, Scotland, Norway
1986 v Scotland (West Bromwich Albion) v Hungary, Saudi Arabia

After starring for Clwyd and Conwy Schools, Mickey Thomas began his long Football League career as an amateur with Wrexham before turning professional in April 1972. He had already made his League debut for the Robins some three months earlier on New Year's Day in a 4-0 defeat at Bournemouth. Over the next seven seasons, Thomas' bustling style earned him rave reviews. In 1977-78 his darting runs down the left flank helped Wrexham win promotion to the Second Division and earned him the first of 51 caps for Wales when he played against West Germany. Thomas was soon in demand and in November 1978 he was transferred to Manchester United for a fee of £300,000.

Though he had been bought to replace Gordon Hill, Thomas was more midfield than winger. The fact that he went a long way towards replacing his crowd-pleasing predecessor, says much for the players' ability and application. During his three seasons at Old Trafford, Thomas earned himself a reputation for selfless running, the fans identifying with him as a trier with far more skill than he was given credit for. With United, Thomas also scored his fair share of goals, his most prolific season being 1979-80 when United finished two points behind champions, Liverpool.

In July 1918, Thomas joined Everton in a deal involving cash plus John Gidman in exchange. His time at Goodison Park was short and marked by disagreements, finally ending when he refused to play in the club's reserve side. A similar position was repeated at his next club, Brighton and Hove Albion and it was only when he joined Stoke City for £200,000 in August 1982 that he recaptured much of his earlier form.

He repaid the Potters by winning the Player of the Year award in his first season at the Victoria Ground. Stoke manager Richie Barker's conversion to the long ball game was a disaster for Mickey Thomas and with his alleged off the field problems, a transfer became inevitable and he joined Chelsea for £75,000 in January 1984 where his old Wrexham boss John Neal was in charge. He also renewed acquaintances with former

Mickey Thomas

Wrexham colleagues Joey Jones and Eddie Niedzwiecki and became a great favourite with the Stamford Bridge crowd. It was here that Thomas produced some of the best football of his career, helping the Pensioners win the Second Division Championship.

From Chelsea he moved to West Bromwich Albion and Derby County (on loan) before moving to the United States for eighteen months and Witchita. On his return he joined Shrewsbury Town before a remarkable free transfer to Leeds United under Howard Wilkinson as they started on their big push to Division One. However, injuries and illness restricted his first team appearances to a minimum and he joined Stoke on loan at the end of the 1989-90 season, returning permanently on a free transfer in August 1990.

He delighted Stoke fans with his touch and commitment and although time was catching up with him, he was voted the club's Player of the Year again. Despite this he was given a free transfer and in August 1991 he returned to the Racecourse Ground for a second spell.

He continued to make news on and off the field, scoring a brilliant free-kick goal against Arsenal in a memorable FA Cup giantkilling win and also being the victim of a stabbing in a domestic incident; the following year he was jailed for his part in a counterfeit money racket. On his return to civilian life he linked up with Conway United, later managing Porthmadog

JOHN TOSHACK

| Birthplace | Cardiff |
| Born | 22 March 1949 |

Football League Career

	Appearances	Goals
Cardiff City	159(3)	75
Liverpool	169(3)	74
Swansea City	58(5)	24

40 caps: 12 goals.
1969 (Cardiff.C) v Scotland, England, N.Ireland, W.Germany, E.Germany, Rest of UK
1970 v E.Germany, Italy
1971 (Liverpool) v Scotland, England, N.Ireland, Finland
1972 v Finland, England
1973 v England(3) Poland, Scotland
1975 v Austria, Hungary(2), Luxembourg(2) Scotland, England
1976 v Yugoslavia(2) England
1977 v Scotland
1978 v Kuwait(2) Scotland, Czechoslovakia
1979 (Swansea.C) v W.Germany, Scotland, England, N.Ireland, Malta
1980 v W.Germany

John Toshack showed an early aptitude for cricket which isn't too surprising because a distant relative, Ernie Toshack, was an Australian Test cricketer who played against England nine times in the years immediately after the Second World War. John played for the Welsh Schoolboy XI but football was his first love and he went to his home-town club Cardiff City as an apprentice.

He was the youngest player to appear in a League match for the Bluebirds when he came off the bench on 13 November 1965 to score the final goal in a 3-1 home win over Leyton Orient - he was just 16 years 236 days old. He had always had a talent for goals - once scoring a hat-trick against Northern Ireland in a schools international and 47 goals in 22 games for Cardiff Schools. A week after making his Cardiff debut, he netted twice in a 4-3 win at Middlesbrough and ended the season with six goals in seven games. Over the next few seasons he continued to find the net and on 16 January 1968 he netted his first hat-trick for the club in an 8-0 Welsh Cup win over Ebbw Vale. After teaming up with Brian Clark, he netted 31 goals in 1968-69 including scoring in both legs of the Welsh Cup Final in a 5-1 aggregate win over Swansea Town and was the Second Division's leading scorer. In 1969-70 he scored his first League hat-trick for the Bluebirds in a 4-2 home win over Queen's Park Rangers and followed it with another early the next season as Hull City were beaten 5-1.

Bobby Robson, then manager of Fulham just failed to sign him but it wasn't long before Liverpool persuaded Cardiff to part with him. It cost them a club record fee of £110,000 and Bill Shankly, who signed him for Liverpool, always considered Tosh to be one of his shrewdest buys.

Toshack had made his international debut for Wales while at Cardiff but the bulk of his 40 caps and 12 goals came during his years at Anfield.

At Liverpool, Toshack quickly endeared himself to the Kop by dumping Everton on the seat of their pants. He helped to erase a two-goal deficit, climbing high above Everton and England centre-half Brian Labone to head the equaliser before nodding down Alec Lindsay's cross for Chris Lawler to score the winner. However, his last 18 games of the season including the FA Cup Final defeat by Arsenal, failed to produce a goal. Though he was obviously a power in the air, other aspects of his game needed attention. To his credit, he applied himself well, gradually acquiring more all-round skills.

The partnership he established with Kevin Keegan made the pair of them the most feared attacking force in the First Division. Some of the more imaginative newspapers of the day claimed that they had some strange telepathic understanding. Tosh won the high balls and Keegan, so quick and busy, was invariably the first to reach his knock-downs. During their period together, Toshack carried off two UEFA Cup winners' medals, three League Championships and the FA Cup. Sadly he was forced to sit out Liverpool's first European Cup victory from the substitute's bench. A few months later, his partner Keegan was gone and Kenny Dalglish had arrived. They might have worked together but Bob Paisley preferred others. Recurring injuries were also limiting Toshack's appearances as indeed they had throughout his time at Anfield. The writing was on the wall and in March 1978, Toshack left Liverpool to become player-manager of Swansea City and so began a completely new chapter in Toshack's career.

His first game was against Watford in which he scored in a 3-3 draw. In all, he scored six goals in 13 games at the end of that season, helping the Swans to clinch third place and promotion to the Third Division.

In a three-year spell with Toshack at the helm, Swansea climbed from the Fourth Division to the First - a feat unrivalled in League history. At one time, when Swansea were top of the First Division, Toshack was being

John Toshack

tipped as the next manager at Anfield. But sadly it all went wrong for him. The team he had built began to disintegrate at an alarming rate and his spending in the transfer market meant that the Vetch Field club had debts of more than £1 million when they were relegated from Division One in 1983. In November of that year, Swansea were bottom of Division Two with just one win from their opening 16 games. Toshack resigned with 18 months of his contract to run and he asked for no compensation. Eight weeks later he accepted an invitation to rejoin the club on half of his original salary but results did not improve and the final break came in March 1984.

He was only out of work for a couple of months before he was invited to manage Sporting Lisbon. He later managed Real Sociedad and in his first season with the club they beat favourites Atletico Madrid in the Spanish Cup Final.

Tosh, who had been awarded the MBE in 1982 for his services to soccer, took over as manager of Real Madrid in May 1989. Bringing a more attacking style to the Spanish side, he guided them to the League Championship with a record number of points and goals in his first season with the club. Yet that did not prevent the club from sacking him in November 1990 after what Real had considered a run of indifferent results !

In February 1991, Toshack returned to Real Sociedad as General Manager. In March 1994, a spell as Welsh national team boss lasted a mere 44 days and one game before he returned to Spain to take over at Deportivo La Coruna.

ROY VERNON

Birthplace	Prestatyn
Born	14 April 1937
Died	4 December 1993

Football League Career

	Appearances	Goals
Blackburn Rovers	131	49

Everton	176	101
Stoke City	84(3)	22
Halifax Town	4	0

32 caps: 8 goals.
1957   (Blackburn.R) v N.Ireland, Czechoslovakia(2) E.Germany
1958 v   E.Germany, England, Scotland, Sweden
1959 v   Scotland
1960   (Everton) v N.Ireland
1961 v   Republic of Ireland, Scotland, England
1962 v   N.Ireland, Brazil(2) Mexico
1963 v   Scotland, Hungary, England
1964 v   England, Scotland
1965   (Stoke.C) v Greece, N.Ireland, Italy
1966   v England, USSR, Scotland, Denmark, N.Ireland
1967 v   N.Ireland
1968 v   England

It was a friend of Johnny Carey the Blackburn Rovers' manager who saw Roy Vernon playing for Mostyn YMCA and recommended him to the Ewood Park club. Vernon had already been invited to Everton for a trial but opted to join the Rovers' groundstaff.

The Prestatyn-born inside-forward made his League debut for Blackburn Rovers as an 18-year-old in September 1955. On that day he played on the right-wing against Liverpool and in direct opposition was his fellow countryman, Roy Lambert. Vernon retained his amateur status so that he could represent Wales at both youth and amateur level. By the time he was 19, Vernon had won his first Welsh cap when he played in the goalless draw against Northern Ireland in Belfast.

He was a regular member of the Blackburn side, displaying a maturity far beyond his years. A creative player who could strike a dead ball with tremendous power, Vernon was a member of the Welsh team that participated in the 1958 World Cup Finals in Sweden.

Though he was more than capable of producing breathtaking wizardry on the pitch, Vernon was also temperamentally unpredictable. Having helped Blackburn win promotion to the First Division in 1957-58 he began to grow increasingly disillusioned with life at Ewood Park. Continually clashing with Rovers' new manager Dally Duncan, he followed his mentor Johnny Carey to Everton, joining the Toffees in a £27,000 deal which took Eddie Thomas to Ewood Park in exchange.

In May 1960, three months after he had left Blackburn, Rovers were at Wembley for the FA Cup Final against Wolverhampton Wanderers. Vernon shook off this disappointment and went on to captain Everton. He was the club's leading scorer in four of his five seasons at Goodison Park and was a member of the side that won the League Championship in 1962-63. During that campaign, Vernon, who had formed a prolific goalscoring partnership with Alex Young, scored 24 goals including a hat-trick in a 4-1 win over Fulham on the final day of the season to clinch the League title.

At Goodison there were occasional brushes with Carey's successor, Harry Catterick, who had made Vernon captain in the hope that the responsibility would mellow and mature the tempestuous forward. Vernon eventually left Everton in March 1965 after scoring 110 goals in 199 League and Cup games and joined Stoke City.

After five productive seasons with the Potters, Vernon, who had taken his total of international appearances to 32 and had a brief spell on loan with Halifax Town, left the Victoria Ground to spend a short time playing in South Africa.

In September 1970 he returned to Lancashire to join former Blackburn colleagues Ronnie Clayton and Bryan Douglas at Great Harwood. Together the three former internationals took the little Northern Premier League club into the first round of the FA Cup for the first time in its history. Vernon retired from the game in January 1972. He then ran an antiques business in Blackburn but began to suffer with arthritis of the hip and spine and died in 1993 at the age of 56.

Roy Vernon

TED VIZARD

Birthplace	Cogan
Born	7 June 1889
Died	25 December 1973

Football League Career

	Appearances	Goals
Bolton Wanderers	434	64

22 caps: 1 goal.
1911   (Bolton.W) v Ireland, Scotland, England
1912 v Scotland, England
1913 v Scotland
1914 v Ireland, England
1920 v England
1921 v Scotland, England, Ireland
1922 v Scotland, England
1923 v England, Ireland
1924 v Scotland, England, Ireland
1926 v Scotland, England
1927 v Scotland

One of the greatest players ever to appear for Bolton Wanderers, outside-left Ted Vizard was recommended to the club by an old school-friend and invited for a month's trial.

As a youth, he divided his time between playing soccer for Cogan Old Boys and rugby for Penarth where he was an accomplished three-quarter back. Soccer came first and in November 1910, two months after signing for the Wanderers, he made his league debut in a 3-0 home win over Gainsborough Trinity. During his first season at Burnden Park, Vizard helped the Wanderers win promotion to the First Division and won the first of 22 caps for Wales when he played against Ireland. His emergence as an international winger helped ease the huge disappointment in the Welsh camp at the loss of regular outside-left Bob Evans to England.

During the First World War, Vizard served with the Royal Field Artillery and 'guested' for Chelsea alongside Bolton's Joe Smith. The pair formed a great left-wing partnership and helped the Pensioners win the 1918 London v Lancashire Cup Final. In February 1919, the management of Bolton Wanderers was put in Vizard's hands until normal League football returned and Charles Foweraker appointed.

Vizard played in two FA Cup Final winning sides for the club. In 1923 he appeared in the first Wembley Cup Final against West Ham United and three years later, again picked up a winners' medal against Manchester City. Though Vizard was not a prolific goalscorer, he did score 13 goals in 1925-26 including all three in the 3-0 defeat of Arsenal. He made the last of 512 League and Cup appearances for the Wanderers, in which he scored 70 goals on 21 March 1931 in the match against Manchester City. He was then 41 years 287 days old, which makes him the oldest player to appear for Bolton.

He then took charge of the Lancashire club's 'A' team before leaving Burnden Park in April 1933 after almost twenty-three years' service.

Vizard, who had obtained a BA degree while playing football, became manager of Swindon Town after they sought re-election the previous season. Vizard, who was the Wiltshire club's first full-time manager, failed to lift the Robins above mid-table mediocrity and in May 1939 left to take over the reins at Queen's Park Rangers. However, with the onset of war just around the corner, he never had the opportunity to build a side at Loftus Road. He contributed to Rangers' modest successes in wartime football before taking over from Major Frank Buckley at Wolverhampton Wanderers in April 1944.

Vizard, who got the job at Molineux from over 100 applicants, laid the foundations for future success at the club. Despite taking Wolves to third place in Division One in the first peacetime season of 1946-47, he was not a great motivator and in June 1948 he was replaced by Stan Cullis.

Vizard later managed non-League Cradley Heath before becoming 'mine host' at a Tattenhall Hotel in 1950.

PHIL WOOSNAM

Birthplace   Caersws
Born   22 December 1932

Football League Career

	Appearances	Goals
Manchester City	1	0
Leyton Orient	108	19
West Ham United	138	26
Aston Villa	106	24

17 caps: 3 goals.
1959   (Leyton.O) v Scotland (West Ham United) v England
1960 v England, Scotland, N.Ireland
1961 v Republic of Ireland, Scotland, England, N.Ireland, Spain, Hungary
1962 v England, Scotland, N.Ireland, Brazil
1963   (Aston Villa) v Hungary, N.Ireland 1963

A nephew of Max Woosnam, the Manchester City and England amateur of the 1920s, Phil Woosnam's football skills were recognised at an early age. His performances for Montgomeryshire Schoolboys led to him winning selection for Wales Schoolboys and by the time he left his Caersws home to read physics at Bangor University, he had won youth international honours.

It was while he was at college that Phil Woosnam won the first of his eight amateur caps when he played against England at Bangor in 1951. Woosnam also captained the University side to the Welsh Universities Championship. Whilst studying at Bangor University, Woosnam signed amateur forms for Manchester City but in four seasons with the Maine Road club, he only made one Football League appearance. He did play in a number of Central League games for the Blues and it was something of a surprise when they failed to maintain their interest in the Welsh midfielder.

After graduating from Bangor University with a BSc degree, the young Woosnam joined the Royal Artillery as a 2nd Lieutenant to complete his National Service, during which time he turned in some outstanding performances for the Army XI. When he was demobbed, Woosnam got a job as a physics teacher in Leyton and joined the Brisbane Road club as an amateur. He spent four seasons with Orient, during which time he had a short spell assisting Sutton United before deciding to give up his teaching post at Leyton County High School and turn professional.

In November 1958 after helping Orient win the Third Division Championship, Woosnam was transferred to West Ham United for a fee of £30,000. At that time, only three British players had commanded a higher fee in the transfer market. His intelligent footballing skills were very much appreciated by the Upton Park faithful who week in and week out saw Woosnam find space in which to play. Always one move ahead of the other players on the park, Woosnam won 14 full caps during his time with the Hammers, to go with the cap he gained against Scotland in 1959, whilst with Leyton Orient.

In November 1962, Woosnam was surprisingly allowed to leave Upton Park and joined Aston Villa for £27,000. An instant success with the Villa Park crowd, he made his debut at home to Bolton Wanderers, having a hand in all but one of Villa's goals in a 5-0 win. Though never a prolific scorer, he did net 20 goals in 40 League and Cup games in 1965-66. At the end of that season it seemed as if Woosnam would become the club's player-manager but he left Villa Park to become manager-coach of the Atlanta Chiefs. In January 1969, Woosnam was appointed Commissioner of the NASL and the following year coached the USA World Cup side.

A cousin to golfer Ian Woosnam, he held the post of US Soccer League Commissioner until 1982 when he became managing director of Kick Enterprises - the marketing group of the US Soccer Federation.

TERRY YORATH

Birthplace   Cardiff
Born   27 March 1950

Football League Career
	Appearances	Goals
Leeds United	120(21)	10
Coventry City	99	3
Tottenham Hotspur	44(4)	1
Bradford City	22(5)	0
Swansea City	1	0

59 caps: 2 goals.
1970   (Leeds United) v Italy
1971 v Scotland, England, N.Ireland
1972 v Czechoslovakia, England, Scotland, N.Ireland
1973 v England, Poland, Scotland
1974 v Poland, England, Scotland, N.Ireland
1975 v Austria, Hungary(2) Luxembourg(2) Scotland
1976 v Austria, England(2) Yugoslavia(2) Scotland, N.Ireland
1977   (Coventry.C) v W.Germany, Scotland(2) Czechoslovakia, England, N.Ireland
1978 v Kuwait(2) Scotland(2) Czechoslovakia, Iran, W.Germany, England, N.Ireland
1979 v Turkey, W.Germany, England, Scotland, N.Ireland
1980   (Tottenham.H) v Republic of Ireland, Turkey, England, Scotland, N.Ireland, Iceland
1981 v Turkey, Czechoslovakia (Vancouver Whitecaps) v Republic of Ireland, Turkey, USSR

One of Wales' most capped players, Terry Yorath's entry into the game of soccer was quite by accident. He was more noted at school for his ability as a Rugby Union scrum-half and had trials with the strong schoolboy side in Cardiff at the handling game. One day he went to watch his brother play soccer against Rhondda Valley Boys. The Cardiff boys were a player short and so Terry Yorath borrowed a pair of boots and went on to give a fine performance. He won four Welsh Schoolboy caps as a left-winger and after turning down Cardiff City and the two Bristol clubs, joined Leeds United as an apprentice.

He turned professional in April 1967 and just over a year later, made his first team debut for the Yorkshire club against Burnley. This was his only Football League appearance for United when he made his full international debut against Italy in 1969. He waited patiently in the club's reserve side where he was converted from a rugged defender to an effective ball-winning midfielder.

Yorath was an aggressive hard-tackling competitor and in nine seasons at Elland Road, proved himself a fine clubman. A substitute in Leeds' 1973 FA Cup Final team, he made the starting line-ups for the 1973 European Cup Winners' Cup and 1975 European Cup Finals but in all three only picked up a losers' medal. During the club's League Championship-winning season of 1973-74, Yorath played in 28 games and occupied five different positions. Towards the end of his time at Elland Road, Yorath was United's first team captain and an automatic choice but in August 1976 after scoring 12 goals in 196 League and Cup games, he left Leeds to join Coventry City for a fee of £125,000.

At Highfield Road, Yorath was immediately appointed captain and in his first season with the club, his leadership qualities did much to steer the Sky Blues clear of relegation. In 1977-78 he partnered Barry Powell when City played in a 4-2-4 formation and though they were often outnumbered, they dominated midfield in one of Coventry's best top flight sides. The following season, Yorath was plagued by injury and in the summer of 1979 he joined Tottenham Hotspur for £275,000.

Signed to add a bit of steel to a midfield that boasted the talents of Glenn Hoddle, Ossie Ardilles and Ricky Villa, Yorath performed the task admirably for a season but when he recovered from an injury sustained early the following campaign, he found his place in the side had been taken by Graham Roberts.

Yorath was allowed to leave White Hart Lane and joined Vancouver Whitecaps where he won his final three caps for Wales. The Cardiff-born

Terry Yorath

player captained Wales on 42 occasions and if he hadn't moved to North America where Welsh manager Mike England found it difficult to check on his form, he may well have added more caps to his collection.

When Yorath returned to these shores it was as assistant-manager to Trevor Cherry at Bradford City, helping the Bantams win the Third Division Championship in 1984-85. He officially retired as a player with Bradford but after joining Swansea City as manager, still turned out in one League game during an injury crisis. He led the Swans to promotion to the Third Division in 1987-88 but in February 1989, Yorath walked out on the Vetch Field club to become Bradford City's new manager. The move sparked off a tremendous row between the two clubs over compensation and the Swans tried to block Yorath's path to Valley Parade with legal action. The acrimonious legal wrangle was only resolved when Yorath bought out his own contract. Things did not work out for him at Bradford and in March 1990, he left to return to his old job at Swansea ! He then left the Vetch for a second time amid a further bizarre argument over whether he was sacked or had resigned. Following his departure from Swansea he was made full-time manager of Wales but the following year suffered personal tragedy when his 15-year-old son Daniel collapsed and died of an undiagnosed heart condition.

He took Wales close to qualification for the 1992 European Championships but in December 1993 his contract was not renewed. He later worked in Beirut as the Lebanese national team coach but is now back at Valley Parade on the staff of Premiership new boys Bradford City.

Appendices

Statistical Analysis

Selecting a best team can be a fascinating relaxation but it can also be highly provocative. It is purely a matter of opinion as to how good a player, a man is or has been and no doubt like my selection of the best fifty players, not everyone will agree with my team of Wales' best-ever footballers.

1. Neville Southall
2. Alf Sherwood
3. Walley Barnes
4. Fred Keenor
5. Mike England
6. Kevin Ratcliffe
7. Billy Meredith
8. John Charles
9. Ian Rush
10. Ivor Allchurch
11. Ryan Giggs

Substitutes

12. Jack Kelsey
13. Roy Paul
14. Mark Hughes
15. Trevor Ford
16. Cliff Jones

WALES' TOP TENS

Most International Appearances   Most International Goals

1.	Neville Southall	92		1.	Ian Rush	28
2=	Peter Nicholas	73		2=	Ivor Allchurch	23
	Ian Rush	73			Trevor Ford	23
4=	Mark Hughes	72		4.	Dean Saunders	21
	Joey Jones	72		5	Mark Hughes	16
6.	Dean Saunders	69		6=	John Charles	15
7.	Ivor Allchurch	68			Cliff Jones	15
8.	Brian Flynn	66		8.	John Toshack	12
9.	David Phillips	62		9.	Billy Meredith	11
10=	Cliff Jones	59		10.	Leighton James	10
	Kevin Ratcliffe	59				
	Terry Yorath	59				

Most Football League Appearances for one club

1.	Neville Southall	578	Everton
2.	Robbie James	484	Swansea City
3.	Ian Rush	469	Liverpool
4.	Ivor Allchurch	448	Swansea Town
5.	Ted Vizard	434	Bolton Wanderers
6.	Grenville Morris	423	Nottingham Forest
7.	Gary Sprake	381	Leeds United
8.	Joey Jones	376	Wrexham
9.	Fred Keenor	369	Cardiff City
10.	Billy Meredith	367	Manchester City

Most Football League goals for one club

1.	Ian Rush	229	Liverpool
2.	Grenville Morris	199	Nottingham Forest
3.	Ivor Allchurch	165	Swansea Town
4.	John Charles	153	Leeds United
5.	Billy Meredith	146	Manchester City
6.	Cliff Jones	135	Tottenham Hotspur
7.	Ron Davies	134	Southampton
8.	Mark Hughes	119	Manchester United
9.	Robbie James	115	Swansea City
10.	Roy Vernon	101	Everton

Most Football League Appearances in a career

1.	Robbie James	782
2.	Ivor Allchurch	694
3.	Billy Meredith	676
4.	Neville Southall	673
5.	Leighton James	656
6.	Mickey Thomas	595
7.	Joey Jones	594
8.	David Phillips	593
9.	Wyn Davies	576
10=	Alan Curtis	570
	Ian Rush	570

Most Football League Goals in a career

1.	Ron Davies	275
2.	Ivor Allchurch	250
3.	Ian Rush	246
4.	Grenville Morris	199
5.	Cliff Jones	184
6.	Billy Meredith	181
7.	Trevor Ford	178
8.	John Toshack	174
9=	John Charles	172
	Roy Vernon	172

SELECTED BIBLIOGRAPHY

Who's Who of Welsh International Soccer Players
by Gareth Davies and Ian Garland
Bridge Books 1992

A Hundred Years of Welsh Soccer
by Peter Corrigan
Welsh Brewers 1976

Soccer Dragons
by Ceri Stennett

Cardiff City FC - The Official History of the Bluebirds
by John Crooks
Yore Publications 1987

Swansea City Story
by Brinley Matthews

Swansea City 1912-1982
by David Farmer
Pelham Books

Football League Records 1946-1992
by Barry Hugman

Rothmans Yearbooks